THE PHILOSOPHY
OF
ERNEST HOLMES

The Holmes Papers

THE PHILOSOPHY OF ERNEST HOLMES

ERNEST HOLMES

Edited and Collated by
George P. Bendall, L.H.D.

 DeVorss *Publications*

ISBN: 0-87516-697-0

Library of Congress Card Catalogue Number:
96-85603

Printed in the United States of America

DeVorss & Company, *Publishers*
Box 550
Marina del Rey, CA 90294-0550

To all those who, in their dedication to the teaching and practice of these truths, perpetuate these sentiments expressed by Dr. Ernest Holmes in June 1958:

I can claim nothing for myself with validity, realize nothing in myself, unless I find and see it in you— because I can see only with my own eyes. Here is where there is no danger; here is where there is no conceit; here is where the spirit has no arrogance.

Contents

A Word from the Publisher

In 1989 Dr. George Bendall, Ernest Holmes' most intimate associate in the last years of his life,* brought out the first edition of this book as volume 1 of a series he entitled *The Holmes Papers*. These gather together talks given publicly and privately by Dr. Holmes not long before his passing in April 1960. This first volume also includes two of Dr. Holmes' earliest published articles and a text of his own composition excluded from *The Voice Celestial* (1960), of which he was the co-author with his brother Fenwicke.

Among its many virtues, the principal value of the *Holmes Papers* may well be the unique insight it affords into Dr. Holmes' philosophy and convictions in his closing years. Although he was, as ever, vitally aware of the world around him and interested in new ideas, it is notable—and perhaps instructive—how remarkably consistent his last messages were with his philosophy as stated in *The Science of Mind* (1938), just as that book was consistent with his early *Creative Mind and Success*. In re-reading this latter, "probably for the first time since it originally appeared in 1919," Holmes, writing in 1957, says he

*For an account of these years and a profile of Dr. Bendall, see *Collected Essays of George Bendall* (DeVorss), pp. 1–7, 97–132.

contemplated what changes might have occurred in my thinking during these 38 years, what revisions I might make . . . were I writing it today.

He found

They were few—for Truth is ageless, timeless, changeless. . . . I am more convinced than ever that the Science of Mind, as expounded in our textbook under that name . . . is destined to become the new religion for the new day.

A sense of this is important for an understanding of Dr. Bendall's labors in compiling *The Holmes Papers* and indeed of his ministry, dedicated to preserving the memory of Ernest Holmes and the integrity of his teaching in a time of no little deterioration of both (see, for example, Dr. Bendall's somewhat blunt observations on pp. 1 and 139).

This volume originally appeared as a hardcover edition of verbatim transcripts of the talks it contained. Unfortunately, the reader was frequently at the mercy of errors in the transcripts as well as of the lacunae and syntactical inconsistencies deriving from the more or less extempore nature of the talks. Thanks to Ann Bendall, Dr. Bendall's wife and collaborator, DeVorss & Company is able to bring out this second edition of *The Philosophy of Ernest Holmes*, with the errors and inaccuracies of the first edition eliminated and with a minimum of editing in order to reconstruct some few perplexing passages. Footnotes have been supplied for the reader's information and interest; for these, as in volumes 2 and 3, the editor is responsible. And a debt of gratitude is owed Elaine St. Johns for the trouble she took in marking up her copy of the first edition in the effort to secure a better version.

The Holmes Papers series perfectly complements his written works as the testament and legacy of Ernest Holmes, and it is with pride that DeVorss & Company relaunches this important collection, further exposing to the world the wisdom of one of its greatest teachers.

Arthur Vergara
Editor

Introduction

"USE WHAT I gave you!" I heard from my subconscious in that all-too-familiar New-England-accented voice —Ernest S. Holmes speaking to me in November 1988, twenty-eight years following the death in April 1960 of this great man and originator of the Science of Mind.

I had spent a week thinking what a great potential for the world the teaching and practice of the Science of Mind offered. To my mind, the movement had fallen into the morbidity that follows over-organization: worship of effects, lack of zeal and interest in retaining the purity and greatness of the teaching. The obvious present weakness was a reversal of what had once been a great strength in the field churches throughout the world: a strong element of individuality, but with the retention of a unity that was represented by the principle of "one for all and all for one." Wordsworth puts it so aptly: "The world is too much late and soon./ In getting and spending we lay waste our powers." The movement suffered from the loss of belief and the sacrifice of the teaching's uniqueness to whatever would financially benefit and otherwise suit those involved in the resultant complacency.

One night I put this into prayer, unconsciously blaming Ernest, and then went to sleep. In the middle of the night the sentence "Use what I gave you!" surfaced from God knows where. I went to my office and began rummaging through some of the works and personal memorabilia given to me by Ernest in the last two years of his life when I lived with him. No inner chord of response was struck. Then I remembered I always attended every talk of his wherever it was given. I could not get enough of his wisdom. He recognized that and would take me with him.

I got in the car one night with a notebook and he asked, "What's that for?" I replied, "I don't want to miss anything important as you talk." Ernest said, "I'll take care of that. I'll have Helen [his secretary] type a copy of all the talks for you."

I thought that was a nice gesture—even if he had no intention of doing it. To my joy and surprise, several days later Helen Heichert presented me with a copy of the talk we had had that night. Ernest's gift of his shared wisdom continued throughout the rest of his life in this expression —some two years. I treasured these papers; but in the moving in and out of different households and offices in the ensuing twenty-eight to thirty years, they were scattered to the winds—some in my library, some in files unnoticed, some at home, some interspersed in things to remember, and, sadly, some lost forever. I proceeded to rediscover them and arrange them in their proper page sequence, stapled them together, and began rereading them. I knew this was what was meant by "Use what I gave you!"

Only a fraction of these papers are presented in this first volume, which is dedicated to the philosophy of Ernest S. Holmes, my friend and mentor. I've called the entire collection, for want of something better, *The Holmes Papers*.

George P. Bendall

CHAPTER 1

History of the New Thought Movement

In the first three chapters we see emphasized what Dr. Holmes expressed to me many times. "George, I have talked or written about only three things":

1. There is one God, common to all, in and through all things.
2. There is a Universe that responds with mechanical regularity to the spontaneity of our thoughts.
3. The 11th Commandment of theology—"Thou shalt love one another, as I have loved you."

In this chapter and the next he emphasizes that "We are Christian and more."

THE REV. DR. Barclay Johnson,* introducing Dr. Holmes, said in part: "All of you in later years will count these hours as among your most precious recollections, for you will be able to say that you heard the story of Religious Science from the one who gave it to the world, who tonight shares with us his vision."

*Religious Science minister.

DR. HOLMES

I have always contended that before we can know what is a normal human mind [referring to the MMPI test that Dr. Johnson announced was to be given] we shall have to stop estimating it by our mental and emotional disturbances, which we all have. In all these things they look for the abnormal, so of all people in the world, the psychiatrist—and this is nothing against him, because I believe in what he does—but of all people in the world, unless he is very careful, he might know less about the human mind than any other person. Because in studying that which is emotionally unstable and devoting one's whole time to that, you are liable to lose the perspective of what might be stable. In the *exhaustive* analysis, you would have to analyze, if one out of ten is unstable, the nine who are more or less stable, as well as the one who is unstable, to get your law of averages, or it wouldn't be fair, would it? That is the way it is: it ain't fair!

I wish to start with the history of the New Thought movement because there would be no Religious Science movement had there not at first been a New Thought movement. We are one of the New Thought groups of America, which have come up in the last sixty years and influenced the thought of the world and this country more than any other one single element in it—that is, spiritually, religiously, theologically, psychologically too. But the New Thought movement itself, which originated in America, had its roots in a very deep antiquity. We would have to go back, because it has drawn its knowledge from all sources; it is not just a Christian philosophy, although it is a Christian denomination.

It draws many of its sources from India. Now India did not have any one outstanding prophet or revelator as most of the religions have had, such as Buddhism or Christianity or Judaism. India never had a great prophet or a great savior—never claimed any. Rather, their teaching is an accumulation of generations—thousands of years, probably—of wise people (they didn't even call them saints, but *sages*).

In looking over these generations of the teachings of India, we find a very great concept of the unity of all life. They believed in one God and only One. They didn't call it God; they called it the Absolute, or Brahma; but it doesn't matter what you call it. They believed in one Presence and one Power, and only One in the Universe. They believed (which later came out as a theosophical teaching) in the mind that sleeps in the mineral, waves in the grass, wakes to simple consciousness in the animal, to self-consciousness in the human, and to cosmic consciousness in what they call the upper hierarchies, or an ascending scale of evolution, ad infinitum.

They believed in the theory of involution and evolution, "the spark that ignites the mundane clod," or the divine idea which exists in everything—*everything*—a Something that all things are impregnated with. It is called involution, or the passing of Spirit into substance prior to the passing of substance into definite form to begin an endless round of evolution or unfoldment, cycle after cycle (if they believe in reincarnation, as they do), over and over here, until they have learned what there is here, and then on and on and on.

I personally happen to believe in the upper hierarchies. For all we know, planets are individuals; we don't know that they are not. As intelligent a man as Dean Inge,* who was the greatest living exponent of Platonism, and who probably understood Platonism better than anyone else in his day (he just passed on recently while still active in the Anglican church in England), said it didn't seem strange; it was rather rational to accept that all planetary bodies are individuals. Now, whether they are or not doesn't make any difference; I don't know; that is part of their teaching. If you would like to take the time to read the best single volume on what real Hinduism is, the ancient teachings of the Bhagavad Gita, the Upanishads, and the Vedas, you will find it in one volume of about 900 pages—we have it, and you can probably get it out of the library, called *The Life Divine*, by Aurobindo.† He was considered by both Tagore‡ and Mahatma Gandhi§ as the greatest intellect and exponent of real Hinduism of modern times.

This is one of the sources of the New Thought movement, because the New Thought movement, while it is a Christian denomination, is very much more than that. You do not have to belittle the concept of Christianity to say the Hebrews were nice people and a few of the Greeks had quite a bit of intelligence, since the philosophy of Christianity itself is a combination of the Judaic and the Grecian philosophies—that is what it is.

*William Inge (1860–1954), English prelate, educator, writer, and Dean of St. Paul's cathedral.
†Sri Aurobindo Ghose (1872–1950), Indian seer, philosopher, and nationalist.
‡Sir Rabindranath Tagore (1861–1941), Indian Bengali poet.
§Mohandas Gandhi (1869–1948), Indian nationalist and spiritual leader.

Stace,* in a book called *The Destiny of Western Man* —a professor at Princeton, I believe—said the philosophy of Christianity is a combination of what he called Palestinian impositionalism (which means "Thus saith the God from *up here*," as the Hebraic prophets said) and what he called Grecian immanentism ("Thus saith the God from *in here*")—while Dean Inge said that the philosophy of Christianity is 25 percent from Judaism and 75 percent from the Greeks. You see, the Hebrews were the greatest line of emotional prophets the world has ever known. They were terrific people. They believed that God is One: "Hear O Israel, the Eternal, the Lord thy God is One God"—*but One*. Absolute monotheists.

The ancient Hebrews (and still today; they haven't changed in their doctrine) and the ancient Hindus (they haven't changed) were, together with certain phases of ancient Egypt which I wish to mention, the first people to perceive a unitary Cause. Whatever it is, it is one and not two ultimates. If they were alike, they would destroy each other. If they were unlike, they would coalesce, amalgamate, and come together and be one; there can't be two finalities. The Truth is one, undivided, and indivisible.

But 1500 years prior to the time of Moses we find the Hermetic doctrine—Hermes Trismegistus (Thrice-Great Hermes). In this teaching we find a great deal that Moses taught (because Moses was educated in the Egyptian court, in the Egyptian temples. He was brought up by the Egyptian priests, the hierarchy of nobility), and he was a "top guy," as history has shown.

*Walter T. Stace, educator and writer.

We find in the Greeks a rehearsal of the Hermetic teaching, particularly in their concept of what Emerson* called the Law of Parallels and Swedenborg† called the Law of Correspondences, because the Hermetic teaching had said, "As above, so beneath; as beneath, so above." What is true on one plane is true on all—which really means (and this is where we got the idea) that for every visible thing there is an invisible pattern to which the visible is attached.

One of the latest words in modern physics I read within the last two or three years is a book on an explanation of Einstein and Eddington‡ by a very prominent man (accepted by both of these people), in which he said, "Modern physics has become metaphysics"; and the view of the physical universe (which we used to call the material universe) in modern physics is that what we see is not a thing in itself. Whether it is a mountain or a planet or a wart on our finger, it is more like shadow cast by an invisible substance. Isn't that interesting? The Bible says, "We see now as through a glass darkly." It says, "The things that are seen are not made of the things which do appear, . . . he shall count the things that are as though they were not."

This Law of Parallels which Emerson said he believed in—for he said, "Nature has but two laws, but she plays the familiar tune over and over again"—is Hermetic. That would be in line with concepts of Swedenborg where he said, "There is the celestial correspondent to every terres-

*Ralph Waldo Emerson (1803–1882), American essayist and poet.
†Emanuel Swedenborg (1688–1772), Swedish scientist, philosopher, and religious writer.
‡Sir Arthur Eddington (1882–1944), English astronomer.

trial thing." And the Bible says, "How is it that the dead are raised up and with what body do they come? . . . There are bodies celestial and bodies terrestrial. . . . so also is the resurrection of the dead. . . . The body is sown in weakness, it is raised in power; it is sown a natural body, it is raised a spiritual body. For there is both a natural body and a spiritual body."

And Plotinus,* whom Inge called "the king of the intellectual mystics of the ages," said that every organ in the physical body is attached to a cosmic pattern. Now, you see: the pattern is generic, the organ is individualized. A generic pattern means a universal pattern. There is a pattern of man—not the individual but the generic or the universal. This is what is meant by "Christ" and by "Buddha" and by the "illumined," the "one Son," whom, Eckhart† said, "God is forever begetting, and He is begetting him in me now."

Every organ, Plotinus said, is attached to its pattern, and when by reason of any fact it seems to become detached, it gets in pain and longs to get back. Augustine,‡ speaking of it in a different way and with a different motivation, said, "Thou hast made us, Thine we are, and our hearts are restless till they find repose in Thee."

Probably 50 percent of the best philosophy in the Catholic church came from Augustine, and he was continuously referring, as Eckhart did, to whom they called "the pagan philosophers," by whom they meant the Greeks—because the Greeks produced the greatest line

*A.D. 205–270, Roman (Egypt.-born) philosopher.
†Johannes Eckhart (1260?–1327), German mystic.
‡St. Augustine of Hippo (354–430), Church Father and bishop of Hippo.

of intellectual thinkers the world has ever known. The Hebrews produced the greatest line of emotional prophets the world has ever known. And it is an interesting thing that the philosophy of Christianity is a combination of the two, isn't it? Observe Greek art and see how perfect it is. You will not find a piece of Greek sculpture, unless it is something running, where it doesn't have to overcome the gravitational balance and attraction; but if you could draw a line right straight through the center, you would find it is in absolute balance, as is all their architecture—but it is an intellectual concept, it is kind of cold; yet it is beautiful.

Then look at Roman art: it is all warmth and color but grotesque in form, isn't it? You know, all these guys who painted the pictures of the little Madonna and Jesus— Jesus looks like a strange creature, to say the least. Four times as big as a baby ought to be, and legs as big as an elephant's.

We have to put all these things together—art, science, philosophy, and religion—to find out what makes it tick. No one system, no one teacher, no one person has given the world what it knows. It is very significant, because this is what Religious Science stands for.

So we have Buddhism, which plays an important role in the New Thought movement. Just as Christianity is a combination of the Hebrews and Greeks—drawing much through Egypt, because Hermes was an Egyptian—so Buddhism stems from Hinduism. It is rather an interesting thing, you know, Buddha's history—it was a heretical teaching in India. He was a Hindu. He was born a prince, and his father would never let him go out in the world to see the horrors, poverty, and death. But one day he got out and saw them, and then he went out to try and find out what it was all about—and that is how he got started. He was supposed to have discovered the Law of Cause and Effect. Whether he did or not I don't know and don't care. All I want to know is, does it work and can we get it or use it? There is a utilitarianism; we must be practical. I say we are practical idealists and realistic transcendentalists. I think of us as that.

He, sitting there at the Banyan tree or whatever tree it was, had tried both paths. He found asceticism didn't work, because he became emaciated and fell over almost dead, and someone had to take care of him. He followed what he called the Middle Path; as he sat in contemplation, there was supposed to have been revealed to him the Law of Cause and Effect. The Law, Annie Besant* says, binds the ignorant but frees the wise. There was supposed to have been revealed to him the endless chain of cause and effect, karma, the karmic law, which means the fruit of action, which Jesus referred to when he said, "As a man sows, so shall he also reap," and Moses too when he said, "An eye for an eye and a tooth for a tooth"—cause and effect, the sequence; that is what karma means. And Moses said, "The word is in thine own mouth that thou shouldst know it and do it." Annie Besant said, "It is a law that binds the ignorant but frees the wise." From our viewpoint, it means that bondage is freedom used *as* bondage. There is no final negation.

So we get this sequence of cause and effect from both the Buddhist and Mosaic teaching. Moses said, "The sins of the fathers are visited on the children to the third and

*(1847–1933), English theosophist.

fourth generation of them that hate God." There was much also in Zoroastrianism.

The greatest contributions toward the New Thought came from Hinduism, Buddhism, the Old Testament, Judaism, the New Testament (of course), and the Greeks. The philosophy of Emerson is a combination, a compilation, a unification, a putting together of all these things, because he had studied them all his life. You find continual references, if you know where to find them and know what they mean. He had studied all these things and that is why he was so great. And then he had added to that which he had learned and synthesized it. Eliot* classed him as one of the ten greatest thinkers who have ever lived. There has not been such another intellect since the time of Plato, in my estimation.

So we find these ancient sources coming down, stemming from things before them, and in their turn contributing to what followed after them, gradually formulating certain concepts which do not necessarily agree with each other in detail but which, in the main, agree. We shall find, out of them, a synthesis—the best the world knows spiritually, I would say.

I leave Mohammedanism out. While it is one of the great major religions and very tolerant in many ways, it did not have the influence on Christianity and the New Thought movement that others do. The New Thought stems out of Christianity.

You will find the greatest tolerance in ancient Hinduism, less maligning of others than in any other system of thought up until the New Thought movement. They were very broad-minded people. They believed everything is

*Charles William Eliot (1834–1926), American educator.

in a state of evolution, a divine spark which, Browning*
said, "a man may desecrate but never quite lose," and to
which Wordsworth referred in "The Vision of Sir Lancelot," where he said, "What is so rare as a day in June/
When, if ever, come the perfect days;/ Then heaven tries
earth, if it be in tune,/ And over it softly her warm care
lays./ Whether we look or whether we listen,/ Hear a
life murmur, or see it glisten,/ Every clod feels a stir of
might,/ An instinct within it that reaches and towers,/
And groping blindly above it for light,/ Climbs to a soul
in the grass and the flowers." That is no different from the
theosophical concept of the mind that sleeps in the mineral, waves in the grass, wakes to simple consciousness
in the animals, self-consciousness in man, and cosmic
consciousness in a few men and the upper hierarchies.

Jesus said, "I came not to destroy the Law but to fulfill it." Moses said this also, and Jesus said Moses was
right. I say this, and I am right too. What did Jesus do?
He added to the great impersonal laws of Moses the personal touch—to the great automatic laws of karma the
concept that they can be broken at any split second,
which is exactly what the Zen Buddhist believes and seeks
to discover today; and he is right.

The past need no longer be married to the future; the
future need no longer be the child of the past, inexorably
carrying on the sequence of a chain of cause and effect
that binds us to rebirth or to whatnot. If it is rebirth, I
don't happen to believe in that. Half the world believes
in it, but I shall be surprised if they are right. But I can't
help it if they are; and if they are right, I am wrong and
shall have to accept it. You and I don't make truth; we

*Robert Browning (1812–1889), English poet.

are only lucky if we come to believe in it and understand it. It is impersonal. Truth will be triumphant.

Buddha discovered—he was almost contemporary with Plato—the sequence of the chain of cause and effect, and he said it all has to do with the ego. Therefore get rid of the ego and you won't have cause and effect. Aurobindo calls Buddhism nihilism. Buddhism did not flourish in India the way it did in China, Japan, and the Malay states. Why? Because the Hindus had a purer teaching and it had to be the one that stuck. Buddhism added much to it but never replaced that essential, fundamental concept of a system of a unitary wholeness, an evolution which is a part of its process, and the certainty that Browning had when he said, "I shall arrive,/ As birds pursue their trackless paths;/ Some time, some day,/ In God's good way,/ I shall arrive." Which is a nice way of saying everybody is Hell-bent for Heaven and will get there.

Truth is candid. It is a cannonball—Truth as such itself. Emerson said it is a cold fact which we must accept. What did Jesus contribute to Judaism and—if we wish to include a little larger territory, and I am very happy to—Buddhism? Much which in theology has been called the remission of sins, forgiveness. He forgave people.

His opponents thought they had him caught. Today the two most highly trained people in the world are the Jesuits in the Catholic church and the rabbis in the Jewish church. They study more and work harder; they are wise people. Now Jesus forgave somebody, and they said, "You don't have a right to do this." He said, "Is it easier to say I forgive a man or tell him to get up and walk?"

14

Now, whether or not you call it the remission of sins, theology has done terrible things with it.

Jesus introduced this, and it was his great contribution to Christianity, to the religions of the world, to the spiritual philosophy of the ages, and to the New Thought movement more than any other movement. Zen Buddhism teaches the same thing but with a more cumbersome method. Jesus knew there is a split second, now an unborn hour, in which the future need no longer be bound to the past, to repeat itself, as Freud said, "as a neurotic thought pattern does with monotonous regularity" throughout life. And Jesus was right. Can you step in the same river twice? Impossible. It is impossible that anything shall be repeated the way it was in nature—*anything*; because all nature is in flux and a flow. Everything.

And therefore the logic of what we know coincides with the inspiration of Jesus when he said, "Your sins are forgiven you; you don't have to worry over the past." But he didn't say, "Keep on doing it"; he said, "Don't do it any more lest a worse thing come upon you." It wasn't saying you can make a mistake and get away with it—you can have your cake and eat it—but it is a great consolation to know that "all of the yesterdays," as Isaiah said, "shall be remembered no more against you forever." One of the most beautiful things.

I have just finished making a tape recording of the highlights of Isaiah—which I called *The Song of Isaiah*; it is a transcendent thing—and of the Psalms, and of Proverbs (which I called *The Wisdom of Solomon*)—the most beautiful Bible readings I have ever seen, because I took only the affirmative and forgot the rest; the rest is of no consequence.* We do not care why it *doesn't* work—we only care why it *does* work. We no longer care why it is that two and two are *not* seven—'t'ain't so!

So we have these great contributions, taken down through the ages. We don't have to go into the Reformation or Renaissance. You all know about them—all contributed something: Spinoza,† the great Jewish philosopher—prophet, perhaps; one of the greatest of the great, Jakob Böhme.‡ Swedenborg was called the man with the seven-storied brain. Emerson—the greatest intellect this country has had in modern times, I think. You see, Emerson delivered a baccalaureate sermon at Harvard and wasn't allowed to speak there for 30 years afterwards. It took them 30 years to discover what he had been talking about. Then they decided it was good.

Eckhart was excommunicated 200 years after he died, because it took them that long to find out what he was talking about and that it was bad. Among the things he said was, "God never had but one Son; but," he said, "the Eternal is forever begetting His only-begotten, and He is begetting him in me now." That is blasphemy, you see. Meister Eckhart is the most classical example of pure mysticism in the simplest form that has ever been presented, because he is as deep as Plato and as simple as Jesus. He was a great student of both.

The philosophy of Plotinus is the most classical example, for one who approaches it academically, of mysti-

---

*These readings became Part 2 of Holmes' posthumously published *You Will Live Forever* (1960).
†Benedict de Spinoza (1632–1677), Dutch philosopher.
‡(1575–1624), German mystic.

cism. I like Eckhart better. It is so simple. It is kind of sweet and beautiful, like the aroma of beautiful roses, fresh breezes, or morning sun or evening sunset. It has great beauty. He must have been a great artist in his mind.

You all know the philosophy and history of Christianity as well as I do, and probably better, until a little over a hundred years ago, when Mesmer began his experiments in Europe, which were brought over here and witnessed by a man by the name of Quimby, Phineas P. Quimby,* a watchmaker in Belfast, Maine—a mechanic, but a natural philosopher. He was a natural thinker, one of the most startling men who have ever lived. *The Quimby Manuscripts*, in my estimation, constitutes a compilation of the most original sayings in one book that were ever uttered by the mind of man. I studied it for nearly 30 years. It is almost impossible to get it, but it can be had.† Everyone should read it. We have excerpts from it at the book desk. It was upon his teaching that the philosophy of the New Thought movement was based—I mean its practical application.

I do not think Quimby knew about the philosophers I have been talking about. Some people think he probably had read Swedenborg, but I doubt it. One of his immediate followers was a Swedenborgian‡ who understood the Law of Celestial Correspondences, which merely means

---

*(1802–1866).
†See *Phineas Parkhurst Quimby: The Complete Writings* (DeVorss).
‡Warren Felt Evans (1817–1889), first published New Thought writer and systematic formulator of the teaching. It is probably a mistake to consider him a "follower" of Quimby; however Dr. Holmes was reliant on a largely hearsay version of New Thought history.

or says that in the invisible there is a prototype of the visible, all up and down the line.

At any rate, someone* came to this country and lectured, and this guy in Maine saw it and thought it was very interesting. He got a subject named Lucius Burkmar, a young boy of 19, and he would mesmerize (partially hypnotize) him. Then this boy would become very clairvoyant and diagnose disease. He could see at a distance like psychics can. It is all real. Quimby had been suffering from a kidney complaint, and one day he mesmerized Lucius. He said, "Go in there and see what is wrong." Lucius did. He said, "One of your kidneys is practically detached."†

This is rather interesting. Remember, Plotinus said that when the organ appears to become *detached from its pattern*, it gets in pain and longs to get back to its pattern, that it shall be whole; and Quimby said he knew it was right, because this was what he had been told. He had been examined and he felt he had to suffer; but Lucius said, "Don't worry, I'll fix it up." He goes in and does his stuff, and it is done; and Quimby never had any more trouble from it. Lucius *attached it to its pattern*.

There *is* such a pattern—there must be, or we wouldn't be here; because no artist has ever seen beauty, no biologist has ever seen life, no psychologist has ever seen the mind, no physicist has ever seen energy, no philosopher has ever seen reality, and no theologian has ever seen God. All we see is the tail end of an effect, a shadow cast by an invisible substance. But the Celestial Visitor we

*Quimby heard both Charles Poyen and Robert Collyer.
†See Quimby, *Complete Writings*, III: 174–178.

converse with. That is interesting, isn't it? He doesn't seem to quite *inhabit* this house but He does seem to *use* it. He seems almost sometimes to withdraw and then come back again; and if ever the silver cord is broken, as Isaiah said—that is, the psychic thread that binds the psychic or mental to the physical—if it is severed, then that is it!

Quimby started his experiments. He soon found he could dispense with the services of Lucius and discovered what he announced as the principle, in which he said, "Mind is matter in solution, and matter is mind in form." Together they constitute what he called the matter of a superior intelligence or wisdom, which he called Christ. The use of it he called the Science of Christ. He used the term Christian Science in some places, which doesn't matter, because we are noncontroversial and I don't care where anything came from or who got what from whom. All I want is the *is*ness of things.

Out of this and out of his practice stemmed the law and method which probably has been used in 90 percent of all of the modern New Thought practice. There came along during this time, for healing, Mrs. Eddy.* She acknowledged she was healed. She changed the system, she said. Probably she did, and I don't know or care. And there came another man and his wife† (I think it was his wife) by name of Dresser who were healed, and they stayed with Quimby and were his very close friends and helpers. Quimby dies practically in this man's arms.

*Mary Baker Eddy (1821–1910), founder of Christian Science.
†Julius Dresser (1838–1893); Annetta Seabury Dresser (1840?–1895).

Julius Dresser was the father of David Seabury,* our psychologist. The one who wrote the first history of the New Thought Movement, Horatio Dresser Jr.,† was a brother of David Seabury. (Seabury took his mother's name so there wouldn't be confusion.) Seabury believes in this cause; he knows it is true.

Quimby passed on in 1866. About ten years later we have the first edition of *Science and Health*.‡ It has been revised many times. About this time the modern theosophical movement in America started.

I believe Annie Besant and Madame Tingley,§ the two great apostles of Blavatsky|| (who originated the modern theosophical movement and wrote *The Secret Doctrine* and other books), were responsible for the occultism and the swamis. There was a great group of people along with modern traveling psychologists all stirring up thought and modern spiritualism. The Rochester rapping# came about the time of the advent of theosophy and Christian Science in America. Now of course there was a great deal of weirdness and peculiarity in all of this, but *something* was happening. Always there is a weird fringe when things start; of course it certainly looks weird to people who aren't accustomed to it, doesn't it? It is no wonder they called Quimby an infidel; and Mrs. Eddy, they said, was a witch, because they didn't understand what they were talking about a hundred years ago.

If you translate the universe in terms that now science

*(1885–1960), associated with *Science of Mind* magazine.
†(1866–1954), philosophical and metaphysical writer.
‡By Mary Baker Eddy (1875).
§Katherine Tingley (1847–1929), American theosophist.
||Helena Blavatsky (1831–1891), American theosophist.
#Table-rapping phenomena in spiritistic sessions held in Rochester, N.Y., in 1848.

accepts and upon which the atom bomb was made possible—the equation of Einstein where he said that energy
and mass are equal, identical, and interchangeable—that
is no different, scientifically, than it would be, philosophically, for Quimby to say matter is mind in form and mind
is matter in solution. Not one bit. Or for Spinoza to say,
"I don't say mind is one thing and matter is another. I say
they are the same thing." It is no different when Einstein
said, "There is probably one law in physics that coor-
dinates and synthesizes all laws," than it was for Emerson to say, "There is one mind common to all individual
men," or the Jews to say, "Hear, O Israel: the Eternal, the
Lord thy God, is one Lord," or the ancient Hindus to say,
"He is One." Whatever you name it, it can't be that, because He isn't limited to that name. He is one undivided
and indivisible intelligence, consciousness, awareness, law
and order, and action and reaction —the polarity.

Out of all this stemmed the modern New Thought
movement of America. Along came a woman by the
name of Emma Curtis Hopkins. We have her lessons on
mysticism.* I was fortunate enough to have taken them
35 years ago when she must have been 80. She was, at
least for a brief time, contemporary with the founder
of Christian Science. She edited some of the first pub-
lications.

However, I don't think we would ever class her as a
Christian Scientist. I don't think she got what she learned
from there.† She had studied all these things and proba-

*(1849–1925), American New Thought teacher. The reference is to
her book *High Mysticism*.
†Some contemporary scholarship disagrees. See "Who Was the *Real*
Emma Curtis Hopkins?" in *Creative Thought* magazine, August
1996.

bly this too, but she became what was called the teacher of teachers. The Fillmores* went to her, who founded the Unity movement. People who founded the Home of Truth,† one of the early New Thought movements, and the Church of Truth‡ were all students of hers. I was a student of hers, insofar as she had students.

You went there and took the 12 lessons—just 12 hours of talks; but she had a transcendence about her that you could feel. It was really there. She had quite a good deal of illumination I could feel. It is strange language to begin with, and you won't understand it. I gave her book to Adela Rogers St. Johns§ several years ago and she said, "I don't know what she is talking about." Then she studied and studied and caught on to it and said, "This is terrific when you begin to find out what it is all about." And it is.

You have to get accustomed to the language to find the meaning back of it. Emilie Cady,‖ who wrote *Lessons in Truth*, took her courses; so did George Burnell,# if you ever heard of him; he wrote the *Axioms and Aphorisms* and was one of the great teachers. I would say that two-thirds of the greatest teachers who were responsible for the New Thought movement went to her. I don't know whether Ralph Waldo Trine** did or not. He wrote *In Tune with the Infinite*, which was one of the first books

---

*Charles (1854–1948) and Myrtle (1845–1931).
†Annie Rix Militz (1856–1924) and Sadie Gorie († ca. 1891).
‡Albert Grier (1864–1941). Influenced by the ministry of a Hopkins student, among others.
§(1894–1988), American journalist and popular social historian.
‖(1848–1941), homeopathic physician and metaphysical writer, a mentor of the Unity movement.
#(1863–1948), New Thought teacher and writer.
**(1866–1958), New Thought writer.

along this line to sell over a million copies—one of the biggest sales of any book ever printed. Christian D. Larson*—you have heard of him; he is still living and lectures. The first thing I ever read by him was *The Idea Made Real*, up in the Maine woods where we used to spend our summer.

In later years, naturally the thing broke down into groups. The Unity movement was formed, the Divine Science church, our own church, the Church of Truth, and, many of them—all of them stemming out of the teachings of Quimby. Many of the teachers were influenced by him; he was the greatest mystic of modern times, the greatest spiritual genius I ever contacted— because you could feel it; it was all behind the scenes, I think. That is the New Thought movement of America. That is where it came from. We came out of it.

It is estimated that between 15 and 20 million people (this was 20 years ago) in America belonged to this movement. They don't all belong, as you might belong, to one of our churches, but they read the literature, they study. There are a couple of million periodicals a month in the different avenues going out; over 100,000 clergymen, for instance, subscribe to the Unity literature.

How this must have influenced the pulpit as well as the pews, gradually working like leavening and making possible people like Liebman,† who wrote *Peace of Mind*—! There is *The Power of Positive Thinking* and *Guideposts* (with a circulation of about 750,000) by Norman Vincent Peale,‡ a very great man. And then along came all the modern psychologists, as I said before.

*(1874–1962), New Thought writer.
†Joshua Roth Liebman, clergyman, author of *Peace of Mind*.
‡(1898–1993), clergyman, author *The Power of Positive Thinking*.

I want to mention too one of the most remarkable women who ever appeared in the New Thought movement—she passed on a few years ago—Julia Seton.* She spoke to theaters packed, jammed, and running over in the English-speaking towns around the world: South Africa, England, across this country, New Zealand, and Australia.

We owe a great deal to spiritualism, whether we believe they are talking to spirits or not. I sometimes think they do and sometimes think they do not. But those are things that Rhine† has dealt with. He used a friend of mine, the most famous medium in the world—Eileen Garrett‡—and he has used Arthur Ford,§ who was also a friend of mine, in extrasensory-perception experiments at Duke, and now at Redlands University. They all have stemmed out of this New Thought or modern metaphysical movement, which is the most terrific thing, spiritually, that has ever happened to the spiritual life of the United States. We stemmed out of that.

That is a very brief and very sketchy history, but it is comprehensive enough to show, as we go back and back and back until the teaching in its abstraction is lost in obscure and unknown antiquity, that somewhere down along the line there have always been bringers of the truth—but never before in recorded history. Whether there may have been civilizations destroyed (which I do not doubt might have happened—as this one might be, to start over again) I don't know, and it doesn't matter. The soul of man is eternal and indestructible.

*Physician and New Thought leader, lecturer, and author.
†J. B. Rhine (1895–1980), American psychologist.
‡English psychic.
§American clergyman and psychic.

CHAPTER 2

History of Religious Science

Ernest tired of people writing of his life and the Religious Science movement in an over-imaginative manner. When I asked why he permitted this to continually occur, he replied, "If it makes them happy, let them do it." However, in April 1958, at a lecture to a group of students, he took the opportunity to express the truth.

In this chapter we see expressed and reflected his constant belief: "We are a teaching and practicing order." Ernest had expressed to me his feeling that we are "the only religion or teaching that includes all and excludes none."

I NEGLECTED TO MENTION the writings of Judge Troward,* which are fundamental to the New Thought movement. They didn't come along until about 1909, I believe, starting with *The Edinburgh Lectures*. There are all of them plus a compilation on the Psalms, which came out after his death. They are fundamental books, and everyone in our field should understand them, because I would say 25 percent of our philosophy came from Troward. It all came from somewhere; I didn't make it

*Thomas Troward (1847–1916), English colonial administrator, jurist, and metaphysical writer.

up. The thing that is original about us is that we don't claim any originality, and that is the most original thing in the world. We rang the bell just that way.

You will find much in reading Troward, particularly *The Creative Process in the Individual*. And you should read the book I suggested on Hinduism; it is just one volume by Aurobindo.* His section on the Gnostic Being is a more complete elaboration than *The Creative Process in the Individual*, but it is the same thing. Troward's chapter "The Dénouement of the Creative Process" is the same as a section in Aurobindo's book on the Gnostic Being. Of course, Troward did not get it from Aurobindo, because Troward died before Aurobindo's book was written—about 1914–1915 I think.† But they teach the same thing, which shows the source was the same. It derives from Hindu philosophy.‡

Now we come to our own movement. Our movement is also in a certain sense a Christian denomination. It would be classed as that, but it is very much more than a Christian denomination, remembering again that the philosophy of Christianity is a combination of the Jews and Greeks. "The God without and the God within," the mystics said, "the highest God and the innermost God, is One God." I changed that a little and said, God as man in man *is* man. It is more simple, more direct, and means the same.

I have to make certain personal references. I don't like talking about myself. Anyone who thinks about himself

The Life Divine.
†d. 1916.
‡Troward in fact relied almost wholly on the work of Thomson Jay Hudson for the specifically mental-science element of his teaching.

hasn't very much to think about. It is like someone who thinks he owns something. If he does, and cares very much for it, it will own him. Emerson said, "Cast your good on the four winds of heaven. Only that can increase and multiply which is scattered." I don't think I own anything. These are our playthings here. We exist for the delight of God and we will play with other things somewhere else. And no thing and no era in history is of any value other than as it expresses some ceaseless, incessant Urge which presses against everything, that It shall express Itself for the joy of Its own being, the delight of Its own being, to sing a song: *creativity*. That is what everything exists for.

I have to refer to myself because I happen to have been there when it happened—but I consider Religious Science a thing of destiny or I wouldn't be here. I have given my life to it. I never even made a living out of it, because it doesn't interest me in that way. I think it is a thing of destiny. I believe that the evolutionary process, periodically in history, pushes something forward as a new emergent to meet a new demand.

Now that is not original with me. It is held in all philosophy, and every school of philosophy, that the principle of emergent evolution meets the demand made upon it, in terms of the demand made. I think that is the way everything happens. It is the way we got our fingernails: we had to scratch, so we developed something to scratch with. It is the way we got our feet: we had to walk, so we developed feet and stood up, etc.—things to grasp with, things to think with, etc.

So it had to be, it seems—as though out of all these things I have been talking about, history might be ready

27

for a new emergent. Now I don't consider I had anything to do with it; I happened to be here. Maybe I was willing to devote the time to synthesize it. It has taken a lifetime; I have been doing it for 50 years, and I don't think we are any more than just started. Something had to happen.

They said, "You believe Jesus lived?" I say we have an authentic record of Jesus, so I accept the fact. But I always say, it does not make any difference to me whether Jesus lived or not, because something had to be done; and if he hadn't done it, somebody else would. It is like they say, "Who wrote Shakespeare?" and I say, "What difference does it make whether William Shakespeare wrote it or *another* guy by the name of Shakespeare? *Somebody* wrote it! Who cares?" It is beautiful; nothing is greater than the sonnets of Shakespeare. Whoever did it had experienced Cosmic Consciousness.

People are always trying to hang a halo on you or embarrass you by tying onto you something that doesn't belong. I am writing a story of this movement, with the help of a real writer, only because a couple of years ago one of our own ministers, in a sermon, told the story of my life and very proudly brought it to me, transcribed, and there wasn't a single truth in it—not a single "fact" that was true. And it was broadcast, by some public-spirited fool, that when I first started, my mother had been a medium. I had just as soon she had been, but she wasn't. I wouldn't have cared what she had been. There is just one race, the human race, and one religion, and that is somebody's belief in God—and everybody's belief in God. Some belief is better than others; that would be the only better religion there is.

But I did get born in Maine and didn't go to school, because I didn't like it—hated it—and quit when I was about 15. I didn't go back except to study public speaking. That is one of the troubles with this movement. There are certain liabilities without proper training and certain liabilities with too much training. I said to the head of the Department of Philosophy at USC one day, after he asked, "Why don't more people come to these public lectures on philosophy?"—I said, "They don't get anything." He asked, "Why not? These are the best in the world!" I said, "Let me tell you something. You get somebody who actually knows what Plato taught and tell him to throw all his textbooks out and forget what Plato said, and tell us what he thinks Platonism means in his language; and if he is good, you won't have a hall big enough to get them in, because he will speak from his heart; it won't be out of a book."

At any rate, I rebelled against authority and didn't want to be taken care of, so I went to work when I was a kid. What I have gathered has been from reading, studying and thinking, working—it is a long, laborious, tough method, but it pays off. I don't believe there is a real *other* method. Whatever you are going to learn after you take these classes—which is the best we have to offer—or in any good reading you can get: what you will really learn will be what you tell yourself, in a language you understand, that you accept—giving yourself a reason that is rational enough to accept, reasonable enough to agree to, inspirational enough to listen to with feeling, profound enough to sink deep, and light enough in it to break away the clouds. Because there is a place where the sun never has stopped shining in everyone's mind, and there is ever a song somewhere and we all have to learn to sing it.

Well, I didn't see things or have hallucinations; I wasn't strange in any particular way. When I was a kid, I began to study Emerson. I was from the beginning a nonconformist, asking so many questions my relatives hated me—every time I visited them I drove them crazy. I was, fortunately, brought up in a family by a mother who refused to have fear taught in her family. She was an old New Englander—born a hundred years ago—and New England, theologically, was pretty strict. However, she was a smart woman and she determined we should never be taught there was anything to be afraid of. I had to grow up and be almost a man before I knew that people actually believed in Hell. I don't know now what they believe or how they think; I only know this: that anyone who does, if he will ever get to the place where there is complete forgiveness for himself and heal his own unconscious sense of rejection, will never believe in Hell and never condemn anybody else. You can only project *yourself*.

So I studied Emerson, and this was like drinking water to me. I have studied Emerson all my life. Then I went to Boston to a school* to study speech for a couple of years, while working to pay my way through this very wonderful school. The people were Christian Scientists and very good ones; the head of it was a reader† in the Mother Church. Here, naturally, I heard wonderful things. Some

---

*The Leland Powers School of Public Expression.
†One of two who read aloud selected texts in a Christian Science service.

of my own classmates were Christian Scientists, and I asked if what they believed was true and they said yes, and then I said, "I can do it." Anything anyone has ever done, *anybody* can do—there can be no secrets in nature. This I have always held to. There is no special providence; there is no God who says—to Mary or Ernie or Josie, or anybody else—"I am going to tell *you* what I didn't tell the other guy." There is no such being.

So coming out here to L.A. 45 years ago or whenever it was,* I came in contact with New Thought students. Here is where everything was taught—everything; more here in the earlier days than now. They used to say everyone here was a screwball, but they weren't; they were very remarkable people. When you get someone who gets up and moves to another place, tears up all their background, you at least have a progressive person. He has at least found courage to move out of some rut, if it is just to move across the country to live, and leave everything that has tied him there. This will be the most progressive place on earth.

Well, here was occultism and theosophy; they had their schools—much more than they have now. The New Thought movements were flourishing. Julia Seton was here, and I became acquainted with her. She was one of the early New Thought teachers. Many of them came here to lecture, and I often lectured with them after a few years, and I began to read and study everything I could get hold of—no one thing. I started from the very beginning with the thought that I didn't want to take one bondage away from myself and create another. I have always

*1912.

been very careful about that. When the history of our movement is written and understood, they will know how careful I have been. Some day people will applaud that; but it is too soon now, because it is too close. But it will happen.

We happen to have the most liberal spiritual movement the world has ever seen, and yet it is synthesized and tied together by the authority of the ages and the highlights of the spiritual evolution of the human race, all of which I have been familiar with, since I have spent 50 years studying it and thinking about it.

I was always studying; and since I had to make a living, I took a job as purchasing agent for a business house.* A street superintendent asked me what all the books were I had around my office, and I said they were books on philosophy and metaphysics, the occult, New Thought—everything you can think of. He said, "They look interesting to me." I said, "You are an engineer and wouldn't be interested"; but he thought he might. He borrowed some of them and after a while he said, "How would you like to come over to my house and I will invite a few people one evening and you can just talk to us—?" I said that would be fine—and we did.

These were the first talks I ever gave, in two homes. During one of these evenings a lady came to me and said she was at the Metaphysical Library (we used to have a big metaphysical library at 3rd and Broadway, and I used to get books out of it) and she said, "I told the librarian you would come up next Thursday and talk." I said, "Talk on what?" And she said, "Like you talk to us! You are really better than the people we hear up there."

*In fact, for the City of Venice.

I went, and the librarian said, "You have a class this afternoon at 3 P.M." I said, "I wouldn't know how to teach a class." She informed me I could pay a dollar for the room and charge twenty-five cents a person to come. I decided to teach Troward. I had read *The Edinburgh Lectures*. I believe I had 13 in the class and got home with a five-dollar gold piece above my rent. Within two years I was speaking to thousands of people a week and never put a notice in the paper. They just came.

This went on for a number of years, and I thought I would like to see how it worked in other places; and for several years I went to Eastern cities and around and discovered that wherever there were people, they wanted it and were ready for it. I had already started on what I consider our great synthesis, putting the thing together.

It has always been my idea that the greatest life is the one that includes the most—that we have to study what everybody has to say, we have to be the judge principally of what we think is right or wrong, good or bad, or true or false. There is nothing else, and we must not live by authority. We must have no more prophets or saviors. Now I say this guardedly, and not out of disrespect to the saviors of the world. The Gita says, "The self must raise the self by the self." Shakespeare said, "To thine own self be true and it shall follow as the night the day, thou canst not then be false to any man."

This is true. You learn from yourself in doing. So I decided that to kite around the country wasn't good for me; I didn't care for it. I had a beautiful home here and had made many friends, so I came back to L.A. after several years' being out of this local field. In 1925 we took the little theater which used to be in the Ambassador. It seated 625 people. We put an ad in the paper and started on a Sunday morning. Within a year the people couldn't get in. Then we took the Ebell Theatre and within a year were turning people away from there. It seated 1295 people.

Then Bob Bitzer* came from Boston where I had met him. I started him in Hollywood; he was very young. I said we would take the Women's Club on a Sunday afternoon; we invited everybody to come. We had about 800 people. I told them we were going to start their own church over there and Dr. Bitzer was to be the head of it. That is the way that church started.

Then, because we needed the space, I took the Wiltern Theater, where Dr. Hornaday† now speaks—and we turned away many, many hundreds every Sunday. This was during the time of the Depression, and probably many people were looking for help even more than ordinarily. I had a big radio program too, which was a big help.

I want to go back before this happened. I came back here in 1925, and in 1926 some friends of mine said, "You should organize this." But I said, "No, I don't want to do that; I don't want to start a new religion or be responsible for it; I don't want to tell anyone what to do. I don't know what to do myself, so how can I tell anyone else?" But they argued that this was something they thought valuable and the greatest thing in the world, and they finally convinced me—and we became incorporated 31

*(1896–1994), founder and presiding minister of the Hollywood Church of Religious Science, 1930–1994.
†William H. D. Hornaday (1910–1992), later pastor of Founder's Church of Religious Science.

years ago last February as a nonprofit religious and educational organization. The Institute of Religious Science and School of Philosophy, it was called.

Finally I said, "This can't be done this way. If we are going to have a church and there are more people, let's have more churches." So I asked everyone in Pasadena to come to the Arroyo Seco Hotel on Sunday nights and everyone who went to Glendale to come Tuesday nights there. I carried this on for about six months and started churches. I did the same thing in Long Beach and in Huntington Park and Santa Monica and Redondo Beach and other places. That is how our churches got started; they were surpluses from Wiltern services. We started classes, trained them, and so on. This is merely the way the movement originated. It grew up; it wasn't a planned thing.

It wasn't until it had many, many, many branches that I really thought to myself, Something is going on here, this really is a thing of destiny; it is really going to become the next spiritual impulsion of the world—and I believe it. I finally came to see that it had to be organized so it wouldn't fall apart. We have a very wonderful organization, democratic; we are governed by a top board of 19 members, seven of whom are elected by the field.

This is a new spiritual impulsion in the world; it has certain objectives in the world, has certain purposes: to teach and to practice, and nothing else; teach and practice, practice and teach—that is all we have; that is all we are good for; that is all we ever ought to do.

We must bear witness to a spiritual truth which has come down to us through the ages; and if there is any truth, this is it. It is a compilation, a synthesis—a putting together of all the great thoughts. When they ask me how I know I am right—I *don't* know I am right; I don't *have* to be right. If I thought I was "right," I wouldn't be here. But if you skim off the top thought of the ages and it is wrong, you have no criterion to judge by at all. That is the only way we can do.

If you simply take the best all the great teachers have given us, the essence of all great religions of the world and put it into one; take the hellishness out of it; take the rudeness and crudeness and vulgarization out of what was, perhaps, almost a revelation to suit the whims and fancies of people or the emotional emergency of a group or individual—you still won't get anywhere. But if you take the deep thoughts of the ages—Plato and Moses and Jesus, Buddha, Socrates, Aristotle and Emerson and Plotinus, all of them—you will *have* to have the greatest teaching the world has. It must almost be done by one or a very few people, not because one person is a genius as against others. It must be done by few enough minds at first so they will know *what to take out* and *what to keep*; what is *this* one thought and *that*, and *where* they dovetail.

It's very difficult to get a synthesis like this that we have and try to get it out of too many minds. It is merely that you have to say, What is the relationship between, for example, Einstein saying that energy and mass are equal, identical, and interchangeable and the Jews saying God is One, or Emerson saying there is One Mind common to all individual men—? What is the difference between psychic phenomena as they have appeared throughout the ages and experiences you know? What synthesizes them without their becoming ridiculous and a superstitious belief that someone is perched on your sleeve all the time telling you what happened? It is ridiculous.

It is a terrific thing to synthesize the wisdom of the ages. I don't claim to have done it, but we have come nearer doing it than ever has happened before in the history of the world. Therefore, we are beneficiaries of innumerable sources. Those sources we gladly recognize, and we feel very proud and happy we have had sense enough to use them. They must be brought into line— the great philosophic and spiritual truths must be brought into line with the modern metaphysical knowledge of the Law of Mind in action, which the ancients did not understand at all. If they did, they didn't practice it or, as far as I know, teach it. They taught the broad, generalized principles that underlie it and which will explain it—*but not in action.**

Then we have to put together that which synthesizes modern psychiatry and psychology—and this vast group of people are still teaching as though you and I had an individual psyche, *and we haven't at all.* There is no such thing as *your* subconscious mind and no such thing as *your* subliminal mind or Christ Mind; this is all a fantasy. The only mind you will ever know is the mind you are using right now.

The reaction to it is what we call your subconscious, which, instead of being an entity, is a subjective state of

*By "in action" is meant *how it works* and *how to use it.* The elucidation of this, based on the work of Thomson Jay Hudson and Thomas Troward, was Holmes' great contribution to New Thought. Prior to this, "law" in New Thought (Malinda Cramer's breakthrough Law of Expression apart) was "the broad, generalized principles" Holmes refers to here.

thought in a universal medium of mental and creative reaction. This is one of the great truths; because if you had a mind separate from mine, you and I wouldn't know each other is here.

It is Kant,* who was called the Father of Logic, who said we are able to perceive an apparently external object because it awakens an intuition within us. I know you, and you know me, because the God in us knows Himself—not as each other, separate and divided, but *Itself as us.* This is the only way we can know anything.

So the Christ Mind, the subliminal mind, the subconscious, and the unconscious are all only names we give to the possibility of that without which we would have no conscious awareness of existence on this plane—just the down-to-earth practical old mind that we have been using since we were weaned. Isn't that remarkable—that we should go all around and around and come back as ignorant as in we went! Until, finally, we arrive at the simple conclusion: I must take myself for better or for worse. Here I am; this is what I think with; this is what I know with; this is what I understand with. Should I ever be illumined, this is the thing that will be illumined. Have I a subconsciousness? It is what trails out behind me as a result of this; therefore, only this can change it. Have I a subliminal possibility beyond this? This shall perceive it. And that is why Lowell† said, "I behold in thee the image of Him who died on the tree."

That is what Religious Science is. Its background is the *impulsion* of love. It is intelligent. I would debate with any team on earth to uphold that which I believe, and I

*Immanuel Kant (1724–1804), German philosopher.
†James Russell Lowell (1819–1891), American poet, essayist, and diplomat.

would lick them. It is an irrefutable fact, now proved in science, logic, and reason, that the only revelation there is is intuition. We have launched a movement which is destined—I won't live to see it and don't want to—in the next hundred years to be the great new religious impulsion of our day and of modern times, far exceeding in its capacity to envelop the world anything that has happened since Mohammedanism started.

I don't count any of the others: they are too caught and bound by their littleness. Several of the other modern religions have another revelation, another "thus far and no farther," another authority, God bless them. But we can have no part of it. We have to be open. People come along and know so much more than we do that it is just funny. But it will come out of this little we know—what we have as stemming out of Christianity, and Christianity out of Judaism and the Greeks, and back and back. I am convinced our movement is a thing of destiny.

Now what do we teach? It is very simple: God is all there is. There isn't anything else; there never was and never will be. That is what I am. There is nothing else I can be; I am compelled to be That. I have nothing to do with it. I have no virtue great enough to make It and no vice bad enough to destroy It. When the psychological reaction of condemnation is done away with in the world, Hell will have cooled off; the Devil will be out of business; present-day evangelism will have been rolled up like a scroll and numbered with the things that were once thought to be real.

Something new and grand will have appeared. We are the forerunners of a new race of people; we are the arbiters of the fate of unborn generations; we are the custodians of the chalice of truth. But we are not hung on a cross. We have a song to sing; we have a joy to bring to the world, and love and peace and happiness.

I am ready to introduce new thoughts and new ideas into our movement, starting the first of the year, which I think will be transcendent. But I believe we are just starting. I believe that we can do something to ourselves psychologically that will yield the same faith and conviction in our science and our truth that the electrician has when he wires a building: when we press a button, we will get a light. Did you ever stop to think of that?

Faith is an attitude of mind accepted and no longer rejected. No one can accept it but himself. No one can accept it for him; no one can reject it for him. We have to have the same faith in what we teach and preach and practice that science has or the gardener has. And when that terrific and great simplicity shall have plumbed and penetrated this density of ours, this human stolidness and stupidity, this blindness which we seem to be born with, this drunkenness, this debauchery of the intellect and the soul—then something new and wonderful will happen. It is the only thing that will keep the world from destroying itself.

I think we should feel as though we are on a mission. Not a mission of sadness to save souls—they are not lost; if they were, you wouldn't know where to look for them —but a mission that glorifies the soul. Not to find we are here for salvation, but for glorification—the beauty, the wonder, the delight of that Something that sings and sings and sings in the soul of man. "Build thee more stately mansions O my soul,/ As the swift seasons roll!/ Leave thy low-vaulted past!/ Let each new temple, nobler than the last,/ Shut thee from heaven with a dome more vast,/ Till thou at length art free."

CHAPTER 3

The Source of the Power: Oneness

In this talk, given before the Tuesday Invitational Group on May 19, 1959, three months following his Cosmic Consciousness experience,* Dr. Holmes stresses the cornerstone of our teaching: "Total unity: we all are unique individualizations of the same Thing." Reflecting the impact of his recent experience, he also said, "We have the concept of a united conclusion of the deepest thinkers who ever lived."

Many scholars have decided that:

1. Ernest probably based the teaching on the works of Ralph Waldo Emerson, because his father was a Unitarian minister, and they had heard that he had helped his mother to prepare lectures based on Emerson's essays for his father before Ernest was 12 years of age.
2. Ernest based the teachings on Christian Science. Ernest had studied Christian Science in Boston with Emma Curtis Hopkins. He dropped the study of Christian Science in Boston when he was told that only licensed practitioners could pray in public. This followed a public prayer by Ernest in the absence of his Christian Science teacher.

*See *The Anatomy of Healing Prayer*, vol. 2 of *The Holmes Papers*, pp. 129–36.

3. Ernest based the teaching on the writings of Judge Thomas Troward—this probably because of the use of much of Judge Troward's terminology and some of his basic logic.

Ernest often commented about people's opinion: "If it makes them happy, let them believe it."

M ORE COMPLETELY PERHAPS than of any other system of thought, Emerson believed he was beneficiary of this antiquity [of teaching], as did the Hebrews to a degree. Emerson said, "There is one mind common to all men." Now, according to our concept and according to the greatest teachings I know of throughout the ages, the spiritual philosophy and realization of the ancient Hindu system, the Hermetic teaching, and the spiritual teaching of the Egyptians were the same—all covered up with apparent dualism and multiplied deities; but back of them all you found there was just One. We have the concept of a united conclusion of the deepest thinkers who ever lived.

I am not talking about academic psychology or philosophy, which may or may not be right; I am talking about the deepest spiritual perceptions the human mind has ever gained. I have no doubt at all but they are correct in essence even though we do not understand the full meaning of them. No one understands the meaning of a unity in which there is infinite variation; no one completely comprehends infinite variation in which there is a constant unity; they are figures of speech. But real unity cannot exclude anything.

Throughout the ages there have been those who have

seen how real unity can include everything, and there have been those who, unable to perceive it, have denied most of that which they thought denied the true unity. Even Gandhi attempted this system. In his story of himself he says that when he started out, he said God is truth. He then discovered the error of it, the reason being that we all *assume* what God is and then say *that* is truth.

Therefore, everything is according to the nature of our assumption. This has been the error of the ages—trying to explain what God is. So he said he reversed his opinion and said, "truth is God"—because there can be no God higher than truth. The Bible speaks of the Lord God of Truth—and that means we judge the divine nature by what goes on that we can understand. Many modern metaphysicians say God is all there is, there is One Mind, that Mind is God, that Mind is my mind—and then proceed to use it as though their finite mind knows what is contained within the Infinite Mind.

In order to make the whole thing come together, they begin to deny that which they think is contrary to the nature of God. Unfortunately, it is so easy for one to coerce his own consciousness; psychologically, where there is an emotional bias there will be an intellectual blind spot. They are very liable to run around denying everything they do not like, affirming everything they do, declaring this is the nature of God. That is contrary to reason and judgment: prejudice. It is the way we arrive at most of our theologies.

There was an ancient culture in India that developed probably the longest successive and deepest single line of thinkers who ever lived. The Greek philosophers developed perhaps the greatest line of intellectual thinkers. Their system is very difficult to follow; Emerson said that probably not over 12 people at any one time ever understood Plato, but the works of Plato were brought to those 12 as though God brought it to them. I think that is a very interesting saying.

The Hindu system didn't have prophets, never had saints or saviors—never had people who claimed a special revelation or a special dispensation. However, over a period of several thousand years cumulatively, each concept of one was added to the concept of the other, and that is why there are so many writers. Through the Gita, the Upanishads, even though they are different things, you find a succession of writers who have thought deeply, abstractly, and who probably gave the world the most comprehensive sense of the meaning of the unity of all life that any system has ever taught.

The Christian philosophy or theology is supposed to be based on unity that came from the Hebrew concept that God is One. There was a terrible lamentation among the ancient Hebrew prophets. In spite of the One, there was an awful lot that contradicted it and a great sense of rejection. A true system of unity will have to include all there is. The Christian theology and philosophy is about 90 percent materialistic and almost 100 percent dualistic. Therefore we may thank the God that is, that the God that is believed in, *isn't*. Then we may as well go to Hell and call it a day.

The philosophy of Jesus was based on a unitary wholeness. There is nothing wrong with that. However, the theology of Christianity is a combination of dualism, pluralism, and materialism, all mixed in with confusion. They have not arrived at the comprehension of a necessary unity which must of itself include all varieties, and a necessary variety which must of necessity include the essence of all unity. At the center of every variety or variation is the undivided and indivisible totality in essence, while the only difference could be in *degree*. (That doesn't seem very clear!)

If anything is to be at all, there has to be an absolute unity of all life, no matter whether we like it or don't like it. This will include war, pestilence, famine, tigers fighting in the jungle, exalted love, and the most debased passion. We are not going to be able to deny one experience without denying the validity of all of them.

By getting into confusion trying to decide which is right and which is wrong, we set up theological courts of injustice to decide, and false edicts to announce, creating dogmas that are very much at variance with the truth. While we have all these differences in our theologies (they are all good, all part of the unity too), we have to start with the necessary base of fundamental unity in all things, over all things, through all things, and which *is* all things. *Brahma is all.*

"There is no God save Allah"; "I am the beginning and end"; "My name is I AM"; "I am that I am, beside which there is no other"—it runs through all religions. The basic teaching runs through all religions; it is the interpretation that gives us confusion. We are confronted with fear, pestilence, war, famine, poverty, decay, and death. We shall either have to deny all these things as real to the ultimate Reality, even while we affirm them as necessary experiences (this is a very difficult thing to do without getting a split personality; it is like a guy going down the street and trying to walk two ways at once—it can't be done; something will have to give), or else say there is no such

45

thing as unity, there is nothing but duality—which isn't tenable, because you cannot have two absolutes, two infinites, two ultimates.

Jesus said, "If I do this by Beelzebub, it would be a house divided against itself." Jesus understood unity and lived on the basis that there was no difference between himself and God in essence. "Who hath seen me hath seen the Father." Emerson said, "Who in his integrity worships God becomes God."

You find this in all the great, great philosophies; but they brought it down from an Absolute to a spirit, to a soul, to a mind, to a body. Plotinus had these five divisions, but as one was hid in the other, the other was itself concealed. That is, mind, as we understand it, would be concealed in soul; soul would be concealed in spirit; and so on.

According to the ancient system of gradations of consciousness from the lowest to the highest—from the mind that sleeps in the mineral, waves in the grass, to simple consciousness in the animal, self-consciousness in man, and God-consciousness in the upper reaches—you would have a gradation upward from that which is unconscious of itself, as such, but has an element of intelligence and a purposiveness instinctive within it, involuted in it, or put there in the beginning—no particular beginning, but all beginnings. Beginnings are endless, and endings are endless. Evolution goes on eternally in manifestation and creation, world without end. It has to be that way; there cannot be an inactive creator.

That would mean: in the mind in the mineral sleeps the mind that is going to wave in the grass; in the mind that is in the grass sleeps the mind that is going to awake in simple consciousness in the animal; in this mind (even physically) is the mind that ultimately is going to wake up into the human or self-consciousness; in the self-consciousness is the mind that is going to awaken in the Super-consciousness.

The Super Mind is hidden in the Mind; the Spirit is hidden in the Super Mind, the Absolute is hidden in the Spirit.* I hope this is clear. According to the Hermetic teachings: as above, so below; as below, so above—what is true on one plane is true on all. It is Swedenborg's Law of Correspondences, or Emerson saying he believed in the Law of Parallels of the Hermetic teaching; Emerson saying Nature has but a very few laws, but she repeats the process over and over and over again. That is the simple thing. The mind that is in a state of complete unconsciousness (to us) must contain the further push of its own evolution or the evolution of its instrumentality. The Absolute, I suppose, doesn't evolve until it takes another round of experience. This must push on to another: "Ever as the spiral grew, / He left the old house for the new." "In my Father's house are many mansions," etc.

But there would have had to be, for this evoluting process, a prior and continuing *involuting* process. I am not telling you what I think; I am telling you what the great minds of the ages have taught. I am talking about the great, not the near-great—the ones who have given the world the most inspired and exalted thought it has ever had. It is a very interesting thing: we are about to witness the reemergence of this teaching and a more com-

---

*The relation of terms in each pair is *greater: lesser*; here the sense of "hidden" seems to be equivalent to "implicit."

plete acceptance of it, having gotten rid of all the occultism and the weird part that has gone with it up until now.

Now we have to have, along with the evolution, the irresistible unfoldment of an infinite variety from an inifinite unity. Unity, in passing into variety, never falls into illusion itself (or disunion or separation or otherness) but must always contain within itself that seed which, Browning said, many may desecrate but never quite lose—"that spark," he calls it. It is in our own Bible where it talks, in Genesis, about the time when the plant was created before it was in the ground.

It is so darned simple, but the implications are so terrific and the possibility of their utility might be so immediate. Remember, we are not saying, "God is truth." That is arbitrary, because we don't know God this way. We haven't met Him this way yet—and that is very interesting. We have to *observe*. We must not arbitrarily say, "God said this," and "Thus saith God"—we have to say, "Truth is God." This means that, instead of trying to explain the nature of truth (which is inexplicable), when the intellect and that which *is* explicable reaches the ultimate of its explicability (if there is such a word), we have to say that *it is the nature of Reality to be thus-and-so*. If anyone can carry his mind to this point of perception, he should stop saying, "Thus saith God," and ask, *"What does Nature teach?"* because its cause will be like that.

And the Bible says, "The invisible things of God from the foundation of the world are made manifest by the visible." What you see comes out of what you don't see; what you do see interprets what you don't see; what you

48

do see is what you don't see in the form of what you do see. It cannot be something else. The Universe has to be an undivided and indivisible totality, whose whole essence appears at any and every point within it simultaneously and evenly distributed.

Theoretically, at the point of a pencil is all that was, is, or ever will be, in essence. It has to be there, or there couldn't be a Universe. Now, that doesn't mean God doesn't make something new—"Behold, I make all things new"—but that the newness will always conform to the nature of the reality which brings it about. We have to say this is the nature of life—we are justified in supposing this—and the greatest intellects and the greatest spiritually enlightened people that have ever lived have told us so. I think we are justified in accepting it; what other criterion have we got? People very frequently say to me, sometimes snootily, "How do you know you are right?" I don't have to be right. It doesn't mean a thing to me whether I am right. If I cannot accept the most profound conclusions, the most exalted thoughts the ages have given to me, then there *is* no criterion.

Evelyn Underhill* said that the only news we have of the Kingdom of Heaven has come through the consciousness of man. The Bible says, "No man hath seen the Father at any time, only the Son hath revealed him." But Jesus boldly said, "I and the Father are one," and "Who hath seen me hath seen the Father"; but "the Father is greater than I." Troward says, and rightly, that the *degree* is the difference; the *essence* is identical.

*(1875–1941), English writer; noted lecturer on mysticism and religious life.

We have to just *suppose*—because that appears to be the nature of the thing, until we can think of something better than facts, which are the final arbiter of fate, and its conclusion. Remember, when I say *facts*, I am not necessarily referring to physical facts. We now take into consideration psychosomatic facts, psychic facts—more potent than physical.

Some day, we shall take into consideration the necessity of spiritual facts more potent than the psychic—because as the essence of the psyche is hid in the physical, the essence of the spiritual is hid in the psychic.* The ancient Chinese taught that man has three bodies, and you have to get them circulating, all three together, or nothing good is going to happen. We have proved this in the first two instances: circulation physically and psychosomatically (emotionally), where there is no stagnation, congestion, or backing up of the libidic stream, which demands expression or it goes back to destroy itself.

So we have to assume it is the nature of Reality that a cosmic will, force, power, imagination, purpose (not as we understand purpose, but only to fulfill a desire) is continuously pressing forward *into* everything, *through* everything, to express that which It feels and knows Itself to be and for the sole and only purpose of Its own delight. That is saying a lot.

It has nothing to do with sin and salvation, nothing to do with the fall of man and his redemption. These are by-products of life having no significance other than that somebody said so; they have no ultimate cosmic signifi-

*See footnote, p. 47.

cance, nothing to do with destiny or humanity—nor does Heaven or Hell, as theology understands it. They are too morbid and the one great mistake.

So we have to *suppose* this is the nature of Reality, and not even the will of God. God has no will as you and I understand will. Dean Inge in his *Philosophy of Plotinus* said that to suppose an infinite purpose is a contradiction of logic, reason, mathematics, and everything else; but to suppose limitless purposiveness for self-expression is different.

We must suppose that hid in everything is the "secret" of that thing—the intelligence, will, volition, self-choice, creative imagination backed by a power, energy, and force *of* itself, *within* itself, which will project itself. Now, this is why Troward wrote *The Law and the Word*; he understood this. Jesus understood it when he said, "Heaven and earth shall pass away, but my words shall not pass away." Troward placed the sequence of the creative order in absolute Intelligence—its movement upon itself, the law of that movement, and the form that the law takes there. This is the "secret."

Now we have to suppose an eternal and everlasting descent of the Spirit,* in what we call or miscall matter, into form—and an eternal transformation of matter in form back into Spirit. This is the meaning of Jacob's ladder, I think; don't quote me on this—I don't know; I wasn't there. Remember, this is where all our Bible interpretations come from: somebody makes it up just as I made that up, and someone else says it has to be so.

*See Metaphysical Charts II-A and III in *The Science of Mind*, pp. 569, 571.

We make up all our theologies. The angels were ascending and descending: this would comply with the descent and the ascent of Spirit, wouldn't it? The eternal impregnation of the mundane clod with the original creative Spirit; the eternal and everlasting unfoldment of that into the much and the more, going through all processes of evolution—to arrive at what? Here again, we cannot place words in God's mouth, you know, and say, "This is why God did it." These are human thoughts we put in the mind of God; these are words of limitation we put into the mouth of God and then we say, "Oh, my God hath spoken!" and every worshipper sees behind the idol's face what he believes he sees behind it.

Mrs. Eddy said that mortal mind sees what it believes as truly as it believes what it sees. Emerson said that we see what we animate, and we animate what we see. Jesus, with the profundity of simplicity unsurpassed in the annals of all teaching, said, "It is done unto you as you believe." If you will analyze that to a fare-thee-well and think about nothing else, you will arrive at something which Troward called the reciprocal action between the Universal and the individual. It is one of the great teachings of the ages.

We have to suppose the involution not as a time when God began to create; "In the beginning, God" does not mean *in the beginning of Creation*, but *in the beginning of any creative series*. That is different. "In the beginning" of this particular cabbage that we are making into cole slaw, there was nothing but God; and God poked the seed of a cabbage into a creative medium [soil] which had no choice but to make cabbage. So it is in the eternal beginning of things, in the creation of a wart or a cancer, in the creation of a headache—in the creation of anything.

In the beginning of this creation there is an involutionary thrust. It is the time when "the plant was in the seed before the seed was in the ground," the oak tree was in the acorn, the chicken in the egg. And the answer to prayer is *in* the prayer when it is prayed rightly (it would *have* to be, or the universe would blow up and burst right open) and not because it is the petition of somebody who needs bread and butter—this has nothing to do with it. The Infinite has no need other than the necessity to express Itself.

Now we can't put words in God's mouth and say, "This is why God did it." There is no reason, according to the greatest thinkers of the ages, why God "did it," other than for the delight. I think the nearest way we can think of it is the creative urge in everyone. In modern psychology there is an emotional craving for self-expression back of all things, the repression of which leads to psychoneurosis. Jesus said, "The Spirit seeketh such"; "the wind bloweth where it listeth, and thou canst not tell whence it cometh, and whither it goeth; so is everyone that is born of the Spirit." What I am trying to say makes sense; that way I am saying it may not. The thoughts are so kind of big and abstract: a continual descent of Spirit, a continual corresponding ascent of Spirit for the purpose of the expression. The ancients said, "The delight of the Supreme—the delight of God."

Why do we create? Unless we live creatively, we die, because there is an irresistible desire to express life. "I am come that ye might have life and have it more abundantly." Tennyson* says, "It is life and more life for which we pray. / Our little systems have their day; / They have their day and cease to be; / They are but broken lights of thee, / And thou, O Lord, art more than they." Augustine said, "Thou hast made us, thine we are, and our hearts are restless till they find repose in Thee."

There is an incessant demand; we may call it the libido; it doesn't matter what we call it—an emotional feeling, instinctive desire which *must* come out, and *comes* out in every form, whether you and I call it constructive or destructive. There can be no difference in the energy back of varying emotions. The energy is identical and cosmic. It is what the energy is attached to as emotion and identified with that makes it what we call constructive or destructive.

But there is no ultimate destruction. They† had a system of the builder and destroyer where everything was constantly being torn up to be reassembled until the day of deliverance of the ignorant—which is what in our theology we call the Fall. I like the idea of the ignorance better.

Then there will be an irresistible urge from the lowest to the highest. The Id: this is the one who is awake at the center of the one who sleeps—something like that. "Awake thou that sleepest, and arise from the dead." At the center of the one who sleeps is the instinctive urge, the impulsion of the whole evolutionary process, the spark that Browning says "disturbs our clod."

---

*Alfred, Lord Tennyson (1809–1892), English poet laureate.
†Presumably "the greatest thinkers of the ages" (see p. 53).

In our theology it is Lucifer thrown out of Heaven. This is also an attempt to tell the same story—but look how it was vulgarized by having a terrible fight in Heaven and God rise up and throw this guy out. This is the same devil who was heaved over the embankments of Heaven that Browning was talking about when he said, "a spark disturbs our clod." All the poets have spoken and written about it.

There is Wordsworth in "The Vision of Sir Lancelot," speaking of a day in June ("Every clod feels the stir of might," etc.); Emerson, who goes out into the fields and writes the "Ode to a Rhododendron"; and someone else, who said, "It blooms to waste its sweetness on the desert air." Emerson thought it through and ended his poem by saying, "Beauty is its own excuse." Let us say that God has desires; the ancients said God is pure desire. There is so much in this that modern psychology is attempting to prove, using emotional drives. Modern science goes in the back doorway of ancient intuition almost invariably.

Now we have the involution of things, the involuted—but it isn't static. It is alive, awake, and aware. This is the burning bush that spoke to Moses—but it is really any bush we commune with. This urge makes the involution *evolve*. It can't help it. It is the nature of Reality that this drive shall be there. It is the nature of Reality that, during this process, ignorance, even backed by intelligence, dominates the spark, which Browning said "many may desecrate but never quite lose." The great poets have been intuitive perceivers of that which science gradually will verify—the language of the soul. Like music, like mathematics, it proclaims that which is beyond the possibility of intellectual embodiment. The intellect may drag itself by a laborious path up to perception, where it falls exhausted, close to the apex—and being exhausted, must go to sleep.

Hid within the problem is its own solution. This is the perception of the self-existence of all life; hid within the apparent evil is the good; hid within the hell is the heaven; hid within the devil is the god; hid within the disease is its own healing. Any doctor will tell you it is the nature of any disease to heal itself. Any psychologist will tell you it is the nature of every mental disturbance to heal itself. At the center of everything, Whitman* said, "nestles the seed of perfection."

Now let's come to the beginning of the evolutionary process and skip over a lot of it, to *now*. We know evolution is an eternal process. Anyone inclined to affirm the nature of God and the reality of truth who will deny evolution is a stupid person; he is a person who thinks the only way to arrive at faith is through the denial of fact. It is exactly the wrong way; nothing can lead us into a greater error. We must not try to find facts to fit our theories; we may only, intelligently, try to find an adequate theory that will fit all facts that are known. Having found it, we must accept it as a reality as far as we understand it. Every deep thinker who has ever lived has done this.

We do not arbitrarily say God is Love. We *believe* it. We might like to announce it arbitrarily, but we don't. Some great psychologist will say, "Love or perish." They discover that love is the greatest healing power. Without love there is nothing worthwhile. They discover that love

*Walt Whitman (1819–1892), American poet.

is the most salutary thing. By and by, so much evidence will be piled up that the thoughtful mind will say: What's back of it must be all love. Intuition is the self-pronouncement of Reality. Induction is the gradual acquiring of the evidence to prove this pronouncement is true. The great intuitive perceivers, deep abstractors of thought, merely have announced, by intuition, that which, by laborious intellect, will take a lifetime to try to discover.

But here we may assume God is Love. There is an urge to express, therefore there is involuted in us whatever God is. Whatever process that evolutionary Thing took to get us where we are, we may assume; it is an assumption, but it looks as though it were true—that Its whole intent and purpose is evolved instinctively according to Its own nature by a power, force, energy, creativity inherent within the constitution of Its own being.

Nothing is brought there, nothing is willed there or purposed there or created there. This is very important. *Reality is not something God made.* God did not make God, or else the God we are talking about is not the one we are trying to talk about. The human mind must assume the Reality that *is, was,* and *will remain,* no matter what anybody thinks. It *has* to be that way. We may assume it is the nature of Reality—not the presence of God, not even the will of God, but the *nature*—that implies the purpose and will, and the energy, force, and creativity to execute the purpose. It is all involuted in that indivisible Invisibility which is everywhere present.

In you and me is the idea of whatever we are going to evolve into. I don't know what it is. I think there are beings beyond us as we are beyond tadpoles, because I cannot conceive an unfoldment that stops anywhere. I can conceive, however, that there are leaps from certain steps here to steps out there without going through all the various processes. We have plenty of evidence of it and a name for it in science: epigenesis.

We don't have to say, "God is *this* way." We say, "*This* way is God," which is infinitely preferable for people like Jesus. It will account for the fact that there must be a deep beyond our deep, height beyond our height, an utmost of our concepts at the end of any creative series. The ending marks the beginning of the next.

We must suppose that the undivided Will, undivided Purpose, undivided Law, undivided Energy, undivided Force, and undivided Delight (which I think is most important) exists at the center of all of us—"The undivided light,/ The light of being and undivided need/ That everything shall reunite," Tennyson said; "It will make one grand music as before." He knew what he was talking *about* but didn't know *by what* he was talking. He said to a friend, "There are times when I, as I know myself, seem to disappear and this other thing happens." He was still himself, without loss of consciousness.

This is the struggle of life, the drama of life, the play of life upon itself. At the center of our being is the delight and bliss and need to reunite with all things. Why? Because that Thing hid within us was never disunited from itself. "Before Abraham, I was—destroy this body and that which I AM will raise up another like unto it." Even in the multiplicity, the apparent duality, the infinite variation, all is necessary for the delight, the bliss, and the self-expression of this Thing, whatever we choose to call It, which is God or Reality.

There is that which we cannot resist, that which is stronger than all our denials. Shakespeare said, "There's a Divinity that shapes our ends, rough-hew them how we will." This is what he was talking about. There is an urge that makes the chrysalis open so something will fly out. It is even the meaning of death and birth, integration and disintegration, apparently all for the purpose of expressing that inevitability, that necessity, that Thing which even God did not create: it *is* God. And so we say that the life that refuses to create stagnates and dies.

Next week I want to speak on what that would mean to us in practical application, in what we call treatment —because our treatment, rightly understood, is not a will-power which we throw upon the wind of chance. It is not a concentration of the Absolute and Ineffable, which has never been divided against Itself—so how, in the name of God, *can* It be concentrated? It just can't, any more than you can shuffle the principle of mathematics into a corner and sit on it. It will elude you.

Rather, we are constrained not to *believe*, not to *hope*, not to *long for*, not to *pray for*, but to *accept* that it seems to be the nature of all thought to be creative. Some thought is less creative than others; and by the very token of this self-evident fact, there will have to be some thought that is all-creative. Jesus said to capture this mystery; *how*, it does not matter.

This is what we seek to do, and if we can't do it by pure faith—which I guess is belief; most people don't have it— we can do it by pure reason and logic, if we will take logic and reason as far as they will go, without deserting them, and shove them into the background to accept a super logic and super reason. We can do it by induction, through the laborious scientific methods of deduction—or by the flight of fantasy, of the imagination.

Evelyn Underhill referred to "the doorway of that little gate, up here somewhere, through which intuition passes." We may do it as certain groups of people over a period of thousands of years did it—by combining all methods until at last it is essential that we accept certain self-evident facts and need no longer even have faith in them, but rather pass to the faith *of* the fact, rather than the faith *in* it.

Let's try that—and know we are one with the eternal and ineffable Presence, divine Spirit. We are one with all the love and beauty and peace and presence and power that there is in the Universe. It is what we are: "Thou hast made us; Thine we are"; and "we are that which Thou art, and Thou art that which we are." There is one Life, that Life is God, that Life is our life, that Life is perfect— infinite and eternal peace, ineffable beauty, stillness, silence, tranquility—the peace of That which everywhere is but does not move, but all movement takes place in It, the limitless strength of that Force and Energy that supports the Universe, upholding Its own creation in cosmic harmony—the Love which eternally gives of Itself through the outpouring of Its own spirit, to the delight of Its own soul and the expression of Its own will and the joy of beholding. With all this we identify ourselves; with all this we align ourselves in simplicity. Nor shall the mind contradict. That which affirms itself shall be united.

CHAPTER 4

The Power of the Individual

Ernest emphasizes here* that we all have the unlimited potential of God; for "God in us, as us, *is* us." By this awareness,
we can affect all areas of our life for the better.

Recognition of a universal God and a universal Mind, which
we express, so that we are living, loving, worthy expressions
of God: this confirms to all of us the personalness of God and
the Universe in which we live.

This chapter emphasizes the divine pattern underlying all
Creation.

THE HINDU SAYS we are saved by works—that every
man is, as Browning said, "a god though in the
germ." Through the process of involution, the divine
creative spark has impregnated the mundane clod which
now has the impulsion, ad infinitum, to evolve—the mind
that sleeps in the mineral, waves in the grass, wakes to
simple consciousness in animals, to self-consciousness in
man, and to God-consciousness in the upper hierarchies,
all of which I believe.

*April 23, 1958.

Dean Inge, the greatest of modern Platonists and the greatest expositor of the philosophy of Plotinus who ever lived, said that there is no such thing as an infinite purpose—it would be a contradiction of logic and mathematics; that there can be no eternity snipped off at either end; and that it doesn't seem at all strange that the planets might be people.

Now what has all this to do with being saved by grace? It has everything to do with it. We cannot take an arbitrary viewpoint; we have to put it together to find out the reality, so far as I can see, in these two great streams of consciousness. It is something that Jesus did: he put them together and never denied them.* He said, "I came not to destroy but . . . to fulfill." He added, to the impersonality of Moses and the Hindus and the Buddhists, a concept of the immediacy of a Personalness in the Universe.

Arthur Compton,† in a little book called *Freedom of Man*, said that modern physics has found nothing to deny the concept of a universal mind, which is, in a sense, the parent mind of the human. St. Augustine said, "Thou hast made us, thine we are, and our hearts are restless till they find repose in Thee." He gave the Catholic church the major part of its greatest philosophy, which itself was derived from the Greeks, the Hebrews, and the ancient Hermetic teachings. You will find it running down through the teaching of the Old Testament and the Greeks.

Here is a philosophy of "the mind that sleeps in the mineral, waves in the grass" from India and from Bud-

---

*The two are presumably the Law and the Presence, the impersonal and the personal; also evolution and involution.
†(1892–1962), American physicist.

dhism. Buddhism was an offshoot of Hinduism; it moved over into China, although it never flourished there as it did in other places. It was not as grand a concept as ancient Hinduism. It had a certain element of nihilism in it, which, Aurobindo says, makes it a nihilistic philosophy entirely. We have the concept of the Divine impregnating the mundane clod, which in our Bible is referred to as Lucifer thrown from Heaven, falling like a flaming sword. Browning says, "a spark disturbs our clod."

Now this teaching means—and this is true Hinduism and true Buddhism—that everything is impregnated by That which is alive and awake and aware of everything, from a grain of sand to an archangel, from an ant hill to a planet; that everything we call individual is not individual by separation, but *individuated* as a self-expression of the totality of all things. That is why Jesus said, "Who hath seen me hath seen the Father" and Emerson said, "Who in his integrity worships God becomes God."

This is the reciprocal action between the Universal and the individual. Troward said that since we are It in manifestation, and It is all there is (these are not his exact words), when I see It, it is It seeing me, at the level of my seeing It. This can go on and on without ever reaching a point of saturation, world without end—probably the greatest single spiritual teaching the world has ever had. Troward did not give it to us, but he clarified it. Jesus said, "Who hath seen me hath seen the Father."

Now, we have this idea of a universe that is alive, awake, and aware, not a dead universe, not a material universe. Mrs. Eddy would not have used the Scientific Statement of Being* had she been living today; she was

---

*In her *Science & Health*, p. 468.

a smart woman. "There is no life, truth, intelligence or substance in matter": there isn't any physicist living who believes in a material universe any more. But the sum total of it, the meaning, would be just the same. The practical application would be just the same in everything which responds—in everything an individuation of the totality of all things, being infinite variations of individuation without there ever being any such thing as an individual anything in the Universe.

I hope that is clear; there is all the difference in the world. If you have an *individual* in the Universe, it will be separated form everything else. If you have an *individuation* of all things, in all things, behind everything is the potential of all things. Therefore, the evolution is anything that is the potential of all things; it will be forever upward, outward, spiral, ever more and never less itself; there would never be any limit.

You couldn't do that if all things were individual. If all things were individual, we could not talk to each other, we could not know each other was here. We are able to talk to each other, as Kant said, because *we have an intuitive perception in a field of unitary wholeness*. In other words, I can see the mountains because they exist in the Mind which is me. We can know each other because we are *individuations* of the one Mind.

Now, a principle does not evolve but is that which is back of our evolution. Our evolution is merely catching up with that which is involuted—becoming aware of itself and catching up with the principle in the presence of its own being. By experience, it extends itself further and further out into a cosmic territory, which is without limit and which must contain all things.

Each individuation has back of it the whole works; all of God is potential in everybody. "Who in his integrity worships God will become God." "Act as though I am and I will be." The Talmud says, "God will doubly guide the already guided." Isn't that interesting! Jesus said the same thing—probably got it from the ancient teaching; it doesn't matter. He said, "To him who hath shall be given; from who hath not, shall be taken away even that which he hath." That is a tough statement: if you have, the Universe will give you more; if you haven't anything, it will kick your teeth out. Tennyson said, speaking of the evolutionary process, "so careful of the type it seems, so careless of the single life."

The theory is, then, that the single life is the monad—the original thing that impregnates the mundane clod, putting into it the seed of self-existence, self-evolution, perpetual life, eternal unfoldment, limitless expansion. Browning said, "a god though in the germ": "Therefore I summon age/ To grand youth's heritage;/ For having served its term,/ Thence shall I pass, approved,/ A man; for I removed,/ From the developed brute,/ A god though in the germ." It is from *Rabbi Ben Ezra*.

This seems a lot of not much in particular. It really has a point somewhere, if I can expose it. It is from the standpoint of one of the oldest and most perfect systems of thought the world has ever known, one of the most comprehensive. We have the concept that we are saved by works. Why? Because here is the thing: it doesn't say work out your salvation with fear and trembling, as our Bible does. (Whoever wrote that was feeling badly.)

So here is the possibility of all things, neatly wrapped up in a little package, laid down in a hunk of clay, and let alone to discover itself. It may be an arbitrary propulsion and impulsion to be compelled to arrive at a certain stage of evolution, which would stop in its impulsion toward evolution as soon as the evolving instrumentality knew it was not its environment; or knew itself separate from it; or knew itself, recognized "I am here"; knew *something*, looking at things, and was not lost in its landscape.

Now, from that time on, nothing has happened to the evolving seed of perfection. Wigan* says of these original genes—those things which are handed from generation to generation, as though God brought them in the Ark of the Covenant—that nothing can destroy them; they are Life itself. Genesis says that the plant was in the seed before the seed was in the earth. All of this means: within us is self-existence, self-perpetuation, self-energy, self-knowing. "The self must raise the self by the self." "Behold I stand at the door and knock; I wait." "Whosoever will, may come." There is nothing there, then, that would force that evolution beyond the point of self-perception. Therefore they rightly say, "The self must raise the self by the self."

Now the Christian philosophy says we are saved by grace. *Grace* means the givingness of God. *Works* means that which is earned. *Faith* means that which is given. "By Moses came the law; by Christ came grace." Then someone says, "Is the law of no avail? God forbid." This person understood there must be both law and grace—both givingness and usingness (if there is such a word). Every individual must have within himself the ability to work

*Arthur L. Wigan, American neurophysicist.

out his own salvation. Life itself has imparted itself to him by givingness, which theologically interpreted is grace. It is all right. What they meant is: *it is all right.*

I think we combine both, undoubtedly; we did not make our life; we don't even make our own liver or anything else. We, in certain sense, do not create anything. God is the thing He creates. "I am . . . beside which there is none other." Therefore there is, within us, that germ of life which is indestructible, uncreated—that still creates. There would have to be. Only the uncreated can create, it seems to me; only the unmanifest can manifest; only that which is not spoken can be said. Now that sounds screwy, but you know what I mean. I believe it is true.

Kettering* said, "Every invention is an intuition, and the continuation of the techniques and furtherance of it is just a series of intuitions." Now, there is within each one of us, then, not only a presentation of the Infinite— "Who hath seen me hath seen the Father, yet the Father is greater than I"; there is also that which perpetuates; there is that which extends itself; there is that which the Self knows. "The self must raise the self by the self"; and it is the gift of life—we didn't make it. By grace, then, or by divine givingness, we receive life; by works, we use it. We shall combine the two, because they are two great perceptions of our relationship to reality.

But there is, within each one of us, a divine pattern. I do not know what it looks like; I do not know what anything perfect looks like, nor does anyone else. As I suggested last week, it is my conviction; I have been spending

*Charles Kettering (1876–1958), American electrical engineer.

hours thinking about this one thing. I try to put every fact I know together—synthesize it and see what comes up out of the pot. It seems to me that is the way we learn things —even truths that are self-evident; they *would* be self-apparent if we saw them; but we see as through a glass darkly.

I suggested last week that I have been trying to figure out what is illusion, what is real; what is so, what isn't so. God is not laboring under an illusion; "God is not mocked," nor is reality profaned; truth never suffers shocks; "truth crushed to earth will rise again." No one has ever sinned against God. It is impossible. Did you know the teachers in the Catholic church do not believe God sees or knows evil?

There is, in us, that thing which belongs to the Universe. "At the center of everything nestles the seed of perfection," Whitman said. Browning said: "in loosening this imprisoned splendor"; Emerson said, "We are beneficiaries of the divine fact." The Bible says, "God made man perfect, but he has sought out many inventions." Now, we are already perfect; we don't look it or act it; we don't seem to be; we don't understand how we could be or that we are; this we do not know. This is the ignorance.

I like Aurobindo's concept of the great ignorance rather than sin and salvation, the fall and redemption—which is pretty finite stuff, and which comes up out of the Christian theology. Ignorance has a broader sweep to it. Here are ignorance and its consequences; "there is no sin but a mistake and no punishment but a consequence." Emerson said ignorance is the only sin there is, enlightenment the only salvation. "The self must raise the self by the self." But the self is there; we didn't put it there. That is your grace—that is your givingness. But by the very nature of reality, we cannot understand it until we see it as it is, and we cannot see it as it is until we understand it. Isn't that terrible!

"Beloved, now are we the sons of God"—that is a statement of being—"and it doth not yet appear what we shall be; but we know that, when he shall appear, we shall be like him; for we shall see him as he is. And every man that hath this hope in him purifieth himself, even as he is pure."* Now, this is not referring to Jesus. It is referring to what the Hebrews called the Messiah, the Buddhists called the Buddha, the Hindus called the Atman, and we call the Christ—"Christ in us, the hope of glory."

It refers to the spiritual principle and presence of "the spark that ignites our clod," or the pattern which is given (this is "the Lamb slain from the foundation of the world"). "And the veil of the temple was rent at the least breath of the outgoing soul": now, this is a symbol—the symbol of when that which is human completely gives way to the divine. There is the temple: "Know ye not that ye are the temple of God?" The veil that stands between the face of Reality and what we have seen (which is too unreal) is rent, and we "see him as he is." "We do not know what we shall be; but when he appears, we shall be like him."

"When he shall appear . . . we shall see him as he is": we cannot see him as he is until he appears; he can't appear until we see him. We are between the Devil and deep blue sea. Everything is, of course, the result of the self-combustion of the Universe; it has to be. This is our greatest trouble as metaphysicians: that we are still deal-

*1 John 3:2,3.

ing in our minds with a material universe or with a universe separated from a fluidity. Or as Emerson said, "We see it as a solid fact, God as liquid law." That is our great trouble. We think we are spiritualizing matter or materializing spirit and that mind is influencing or controlling something that is not mind.

Now, if we would follow Einstein's equation, we would not do that: we would merely apply it through a law of parallels of the kind where he says energy and mass are equal, identical, and interchangeable—they are the same thing. Mrs. Eddy said, "All is Mind and Its infinite manifestation, and God is All-in-all." Spinoza said, "I do not say mind is one thing and matter is another; I say they are the same thing." Quimby said, "Mind is matter in solution, matter is mind in form." The Bible says, "the invisible things of God, from the foundation of the universe, are made manifest or known by the visible."

All it means is that what you see comes out of what you don't see; what you don't see must have* the pattern of what you do see; if you should [truly] see what you do see, then what you don't see you would see, and it would be what you do see.† Then "when he shall appear, we shall be like him; for we shall see him as he is." But he cannot appear until we see him as he is.

Our vision is cast at a lower level; it is beclouded, as through a glass darkly, by some kind of psychological projection we hang up—the pattern of what we think—in front of the Universe we *think* it is. And looking at the Universe it *is*, we see only the Universe we *think*—which

---

* = hold.
† "Don't see" relates to substance, reality; "do see" relates to immediate appearance.

is a projection. Our thinking doesn't change reality at all. Some people think it does; but it never flattened the world when they thought it was flat—it only flattened their experience on a round one. When someone knew it was round, he could navigate it.

Now there must be in here (symbolically at the center of man's being) a pattern which is perfect. What we see has to be attached to a pattern which is perfect or there wouldn't be anything to vitalize it, just as the gene is indestructible, handed from generation to generation. I don't consider truth a matter of my opinion at all; truth isn't what I think. I am fortunate if what I think is in line with truth. It would be terrible if truth had to be what I think. I did not put the mountains up there. The mountains, as I look at them, are to me what I am to the mountains.

"As thou seest, that thou be'est. As thou beholdest man, that to become thou must: God if thou seest God, dust if thou seest dust." We tend to become like what we look at. The mountains are here, but I hang a veil in front of the mountains, in a sense. We don't see each other and everything as it is, do we? We know enough about psychology, projection, emotional bias, and intellectual blind spots to know that we have a veil between ourselves— all of our experiences and everyone we meet veiled by a projection, by an emotional bias.

There is no way in the world to figure how the wisest, the most erudite, the most scholastic people on earth— the Jesuits—would still believe in Hell except there is an emotional bias in them that will not let them analyze it. If they ever got to that analysis, Hell would cool off. We are looking at a real Universe but are not seeing it.

Now when the veil is rent, the veil of the temple: the

temple is this body. It isn't "over there"; it isn't a church or mosque or synagogue. We call it such, but the temple is this: "Know ye not that ye are the temple of God? . . . whose temple ye are." And so the veil of the temple is rent; the dead walk, and the graves give up their dead. It is all a symbol—something that happens in some degree in our own experience if the veil of the temple is rent. The darned thing won't tear (if that is what a rent veil is; it is one that is torn, isn't it?) until we see it as it is. Then when we see it, it can't help ripping itself apart, because it was held together only by our own imagination. (It is a curtain of concealment, someone said.)

This does not mean that when we look into the perfect, the corn-popper is already there, the threshing machine, the sewing machine, and the breadmixer—it doesn't mean that at all; because the Universe isn't static. Emerson said, "The Ancient of Days is in the latest invention." It means that That which is self-perpetuated, self-imagining, self-executing, self-everything is there. But now, out of It shall come a new creativity. Since It never presents Itself, even in Its entirety, to two persons alike, then out of this, through each one of us, shall come a unique creativity.

That is why Emerson said imitation is suicide. No two persons are ever alike or need be or could be if they tried. If there were two people alike, one would be unnecessary in the creative process and wouldn't be here at all. Therefore Emerson said that there is a place where everyone may let out his reins to the full extent—but he is afraid to do it.

So there is unique presentation in each one of us, if we would listen to it. Emerson said, "Listen greatly to yourself; keep up this lowly listening," etc. Our Bible says, "Be still and know." It all means the same thing. There is, then, within each one of us "a god though in the germ." I don't think this is an opinion; to me it isn't just a poetical something—it is beautiful, inspiring; it is God-given. Life has made it this way, and you and I can't change it. We may only accept what it is. Though we appear to reject it and throw it out the front door, it will come in the back door; it will always be there by a persistency that is completely irresistible, by a nonresistance that nothing can resist and a nonviolence that nothing can violate.

Therefore it is certain that any individual, in such degree as he will see reality, will experience it. It will automatically manifest. If all the world said, "No, all the thoughts of the ages have nothing to do with the fact that two and two are four" (referring to the old shibboleth which we have in our field and others have, that what a guy thinks has something to do with what he knows), it still would not be so—or else what you know isn't so. If when Jesus—it is my belief—said to Lazarus, "Come forth," Lazarus had not come forth, I think Jesus would have dropped dead. The frustration would have been so great it would have killed him.

I find nothing in the Universe that says No to reality; there is nothing in any of us that can. Therefore there must be a transcendency of our own thought that is possible, that has immediate precedence over everything that has ever gone before, everything that everybody ever believed or thought, or that all people believed. "The great are great only because we are on our knees. Let us arise."

You will discover no greatness outside yourself; that

which appears to be greatness in another is merely as much as you have projected from yourself to the other. As that hidden thing is removed, you and I will see, in the other, the more perfect image. We have disclosed it; but we couldn't disclose it until we saw it as it is. And we can't see it as it is until we *are* as it is—and there isn't any more *is*-er than that!

Now we may, to be brief, play a game with our intellect, our emotions, our religions, and our philosophies; we may sit around with our saviors and saints; but they will all have to go out the window when God comes in. They will all have to go out in such degree as the Truth comes in, and we shall no longer live by proxy. Jesus knew this when he said, "Why callest thou me good? There is none good save God." They tried to make him king, and he had no desire to be that; he was a teacher; he was following the law of Moses and adding to it the personal equation "I came not to destroy, but to fulfill." It makes a perfect thing—a Universe of Law and order, Presence and person; and that is exactly what it is. It may be that there is an action and reaction which governs everything.

Jesus said, "It is expedient that I go away, in order that the Spirit shall understand what I am talking about." This is *you*. "I have come to reveal the self to the self"—that is the only revelation there is. That is why Shakespeare said, "To thine own self be true, and it shall follow as the night the day thou canst not then be false to any man." But we are afraid of the real self.

First of all, we think we have to be so spiritual. *We don't know what it means to be spiritual.* We do not listen to children praying—that is our trouble; we forget the

74

spontaneity of it. We think it must be something so profound we can't understand it. We don't know it is so simple that every time we deny it, we are affirming it! Our trouble is we don't *expect* enough. Yet since grace is given, the gift is made, or the Lamb is slain "from the foundation of the world." "The self must raise the self by the self."

When the little boy was in the pigpen, papa didn't come and say, "Come home." If he had dragged him home, then the little boy would have been an automaton, a cosmic robot. Everything in the Universe is alive, awake, and aware with spontaneous self-combustion. You and I or somebody else might (whether we do or not) draw some kind of a picture that was never drawn before. So let's do it.

Know that originality is within us; we are very humble, and there is nothing arrogant about this, neither is there anything self-effacing. Even if this is the only thing we ever know, all things must forevermore remain in relationship to it—no matter how glorious they are. The Universe has decreed it and we cannot change it. We shall recognize that effort, that power, that depth of feeling, that glory of creativity, that warmth and color of love, that song that is celestial. We shall know that here and now God Himself goes forth anew into creation through us. We have accepted the gift of Life and are now playing with it on the shores of time, where the waters of the Infinite wash our feet. Yet all eternity seems in our hearts. We are embraced—held in the soft embrace of That which is pure Love and perfect Peace.

And so it is.

CHAPTER 5

The Definition of Religious Science

Shortly after the previous talk, Ernest had a group of us at his house for a "command dinner." In attendance were Dr. and Mrs. Reg Armor,* Thornton Kinney and his wife, Dr. Mabel Kinney (member of the California State Board of Education), Mr. and Mrs. William Lynn,† Dr. William H. D. Hornaday, Dr. Barclay Johnson, and myself.

Dr. Holmes announced to us that the Governor of California, Goodwin Knight (holder of a doctorate in Humanities conferred by the Institute of Religious Science), had requested that Dr. Kinney obtain from Dr. Holmes a 25-word definition of Religious Science. For an hour or two, we all contributed ideas; but when Ernest announced the definition, it didn't seem much to resemble what we had talked about.

A couple of weeks later, on May 27 (1958), he addressed this before the Tuesday Invitational Group. Attendance was only by those receiving his personal invitation. Guests flew in from Arizona, New Mexico, Illinois, and Texas. Before this group Dr. Holmes sat in a chair and expressed freely his thoughts and ideas. I felt a great sense of humility as the only minister on the permanent invitational list.

---

*Reginald Armor (1903–1977), the earliest of Dr. Holmes' associates besides his brother Fenwicke.
†William Lynn was, as a young man, a "protégé" of Dr. Holmes. He later served the United Church of Religious Science and in retirement is executor of Dr. Holmes' estate.

I HAD A VERY interesting experience yesterday: I spoke to 50 Christian ministers—I mean ministers of the Christian Church, which is rather liberal in a way. One of them said to me, in a very sweet way, "In reference to what you said about such-and-such a thing . . ." and I stopped him and said, "I didn't say anything about that subject," and he said, "You implied it," and I said, "No, you inferred it." I said, "This is in your mind and is a psychological projection—but unconscious—and has nothing to do with what I said." There was nothing mean or bad about it, and I thought how our reactions to life are that way.

They are a nice group; all have churches and are pretty broadly gauged. They have had ministers from all faiths —even a Catholic priest and a rabbi. Someone asked the priest, "How about the Reformation?" and he said, "I don't know anything about any reformation; I have not heard of any reformation in our church." He said the Catholic church has never had a reformation; they are just as they always were. Now isn't that a clever answer? I thought it was.

In talking with Mabel Kinney the other evening (she is a member of the State Board which has charge of our scholastic work—schools, colleges, etc.), she said that one of the members of the Board—and they are all college professors or educators—said, "Will you please write out for me in 25 words what Religious Science is?" That is something, isn't it? So I sat down and wrote it, and it said: Religious Science is a synthesis of laws of science, opinions of philosophy, and revelations of religion applied to human needs and the aspirations of man. Isn't that good? *Religious Science is a synthesis of laws of science, opinions of philosophy, and revelations of religion applied to human needs and the aspirations of man.* I think it is wonderful!

Nearly 2000 years ago, Plotinus, who was the greatest of the Neoplatonists and whom Dean Inge called the king of intellectual mystics of the ages, said that the only avenues of learning we have, have come from science, philosophy, and illumination. By illumination he meant what we mean by religion, intuition. We believe revelation is intuition perceived by the conscious intelligence, and therefore to us *religion* wouldn't be quite as broad a term as *intuition*. But to cover the need of the world, I thought we better put it that way, because the only avenues through which knowledge may come to the human mind are science, philosophy, and religion.

Science is defined as a system of laws, causes in nature, and techniques for the use and application of them to human needs; philosophy is anybody's opinion about anything. Most people mistakenly think philosophy means Plato and Aristotle and Socrates. It means them only because these people wrote or because what they said was recorded. Therefore we refer to them as "the philosophers" merely because they were the ones whose words were taken down and recorded. There have been thousands of others just as good that we never heard of.

I repeat: philosophy is anybody's opinion about anything, and revelation means intuition (which we all have) brought to the surface and perceived by the conscious intelligence. It is back of the psychic. Now, the revelations which have come through the psychic are distorted by the psychic. That is why, when you read so many of these "revelations," you will find them a combination of intuition and projected opinions. This is where Hell came from. (There is no Hell.)

One time, a very good friend of mine who belongs to AA came to my house and said, "I want to tell you what an alcoholic goes through and why only an alcoholic can understand one." For two hours he recited things that happened to him in this state. That was the most gruesome recital, the most realistic and damndest thing I ever listened to. When I asked if that was the way it was, he said, "That is the way it is." He said he would finally wake up by breaking everything in the room, tearing the pictures down, breaking out the windows. I thought, then, that this isn't so different from the poet Dante. Maybe *he* was drunk when he painted his pictures of hell! It comes from the same source—a grotesqueness.

The prolific imagination, bordering on morbidity, that projects itself from the psychic into the intellect is not to be discerned. It has nothing to do with intuition, which is a direct perception of truth without processes of reasoning. That is why you can always tell whether someone is writing from intuition or the psychic. Most people think a hunch is an intuition. It may or may not be. We live in these three worlds of spiritual absolute, human psychic reactions, and physical manifestation.

3500 hundred years ago, Pantanjali* was compiling the knowledge of Ancient India at that time. Have you read *The Sutras of Patanjali*? It is one of the greatest little books of the ages. It very definitely shows how you have to get through what we call the psychic. The Bible says, "Try the spirits and see whether or not they are of God."

*(2d century B.C.), Indian scholar and grammarian.

Now this psychic field is what Mrs. Eddy called the mortal mind or sum total of human thought and what the Bible calls the carnal mind, "which is enmity against God." It is what Carl Jung* calls the collective unconscious, which means the sum total of all the thoughts and actions of the ages, operating on a psychic level and a psychic field that impinges upon everyone—just as it is now definitely known that there is an inertia to human thought patterns.

Joseph Jastrow† said that in counseling and analysis in psychiatry, one of the principal things they have to overcome is what he calls the inertia of thought patterns. Now there is one of our prominent psychologists talking, and he said they act exactly as though they were entities. Mrs. Eddy called this "the argument of error," if you are familiar with her sayings. Quimby said, "We go around surrounded by our opinions. I represent the man of wisdom; I enter the man of opinions; I explain that they are only opinions." Jesus said, "Know the truth, and the truth shall make you free."

We are surrounded by a psychic realm which contains the thoughts and opinions; and that is what we are hearing a lot of now in "regression" through hypnotism. People get caught in a psychic trap which is omnipresent and can be picked up by anyone at any time. If they are clairvoyant, they will see the action; if they are clairaudient, they will hear the voice. This same field impinges upon all of us, and I think in some degree we are all hypnotized from cradle to grave.

*(1875–1961), Swiss psychologist and psychiatrist.
†(1863–1944), American psychologist.

Why does everybody say, "You can't do it"? Why does everyone say, "There will always be war," "There will always be poverty"? Only because there *has* been! There is no logic in it. The logic of experience is no criterion of judgment, of what could be now or ought to be in the future. Every new advance in science can be an advance only because it arbitrarily contradicts much that, up until then, was considered to be true. That is why Tennyson said, "New truth makes ancient good uncouth./ Our little systems have their day;/ They have their day and cease to be:/ They are but broken lights of Thee,/ And Thou, O Lord, art more than they."

I said to some ministers yesterday something I said to you last week: I think that the time will come when religion will get free from its superstition. It is inevitable that it will come, but I don't know when. Philosophy will get rid of its dualism, because most philosophy is materialistic and dualistic. Science, because of its findings, will merge into more or less of a mystical state relative to the nature of the Universe, which many scientists are now doing. When those three things combine, you will have the next and new religion of the world, which will ultimately immerse all religions and finally dominate. Why? *We have it.* That is what Religious Science is supposed to do, and that is why I made that definition with that in mind. Why? Because we do not consider that there is an isolated fact in the Universe, a separate entity, or an apartness from the sum total of all things.

We consider the whole universal system to be a unitary wholeness, undivided and indivisible. Therefore its entirety is at the point of our perception, always. But our

81

perception is somewhat influenced by the psychic background of the world. I mean, these regressions pick up the experiences of the ages. I have read and seen so much of this stuff all my life—because it has been a part of what we know about; and I know this is what happens. Anybody can remember anything that ever happened to anybody whoever lived—if he happens to tune into it.

Some day there will be a physical instrument perfected that will tune into it and record the words of Jesus, John the Baptist, or Caesar. Right now, one who can practice psychometry and really objectify it would take a brick (if Caesar lived in a brick house) and hold it in his hand, and it would be entirely possible for him to describe the house, the rooms, the furniture (if they had any), what they ate, who was there, and to hear them talk and say what they said 2000 years ago. Already in the annals of the British and American societies of psychic research there is irrefutable evidence of this. While it might be the world will say 't'ain't so, it *is*.

I really wanted to discuss the concept that we have suggested many times for us to think about during the summer. This fall we are going to do some very special things. We exist to prove our position as far as the world is concerned. I even had the nerve yesterday to say—it was a question about salvation—"Well, that has to do with salvation, the problem of evil, which you people know more about than I do." It was mean of me to say that. I had the nerve to say that "If anyone was lost, I wouldn't know where to look for him." They looked strange.* I said, "Neither would you."

*I.e. the ministers referred to on pp. 77 and 86.

Logic and reason compel us to accept that the Universe is a unitary wholeness, but we do not stop to think what this means—that it is a *unitary wholeness*. That which is one, naturally, is undivided and indivisible. Therefore all of it appears at any and every point within it; the totality of infinity is whatever you are thinking. All of God is right where you are. The entirety of the universal laws of nature exists between your two fingers when you put them as close together as you can; all action and reaction exists in the possibility of the quiver of an eyelash. It is impossible to shove a grain of sand across the width of your thumbnail without shifting the entire weight of the sidereal universe—that means all the universe that is in manifestation, anywhere. That wouldn't be possible if it weren't for this unitary wholeness. The fact that you and I can talk to each other is proof enough that we exist in a medium which, Emerson said, "is common to all individual men."*

Immanuel Kant, in *The Critique of Pure Reason*—he is called the Father of Logic as Socrates is called the Father of Philosophy and Homer the Father of Literature—stated: "It is impossible for us to recognize each other. The only way we can is that it awakens an intuition within us in a common medium." Now, this is his way of saying, "I know you when you know me, because the mind in you that knows me is the mind in me that knows you." *There is one mind common to all men.*

This unitary wholeness we must accept, whether we understand it or not. We must always remember that we may *believe* what is *not*; so we can *know* only what *is so*,

---

*"There is one mind common to all individual men."

even though that which is not so (which we believe in) may bind us—because we believe in it. All bondage is ignorance. That is why Emerson said there is no sin but ignorance and no salvation but enlightenment.

That is also why the Hindus say man is saved by works rather than grace; the Christians say he is saved by grace rather than works; and, in our system, we put them both together and say: the possibility of salvation—not the salvation of the soul, but salvation from the lesser to the greater—lies *in works, through grace.* Don't you think that is better? I tried to synthesize it and put it together. *Grace* means that which is given; *works* means that which is earned. Since everything is given, we will have to earn the right to use it—to even know that it is there—by perception and through action. So there is a difference between believing and knowing. Someone said, "The devils also believe, and tremble."* Of course, we don't believe in devils. I think he was merely making a point.

If the whole thing is everywhere present, which it is, then all of God is between our fingers. The infinitesimal and the magnitudinous (I don't know whther there is such a word; if there isn't, I just made it up), the big and the little: Emerson said, "There is no great and no small to the Soul that maketh all." We know this theoretically, but we do not know what it means practically. For instance, it is well accepted in medicine that a person has a wart; yet someone says, "You haven't got it," and nine times out of ten it will disappear. I used to take warts off the boys when I had a Boy Scout troop. This we accept; but the moment we try to erase a cancer, what happens? All the

*James 2:19.

thought of pain, of anguish, of incurability, or else fear in the whole race mind, backs up our negation and flows through it, making it very difficult to affirm its opposite. This is the only difference, if what you and I believe is true. The difference would not be in the thing but in our reaction to it.

Infinity presses against finiteness, absoluteness becomes relativity—but finiteness hasn't learned how to give itself back to infinity, nor relativity back to absoluteness. Therefore it considers itself *apart* and *separate* and *other than*—and not *one with*. We say we are one *with* God and one *in* God. This is a mistake; we are one *of* whatever the nature of God is. Whatever it is, it is *one*. All the great have said it; I didn't make it up. The Hindus say, "He is all"; the Hebrews say, "God is One." It is all the same thing.

Now, you see, that which the intellect may perceive, logic may accept, and rationalization (that which is rational) cannot deny. Like an axiom, it is a self-evident truth that rationality and sanity cannot deny—but they *do* deny its implication. We think it is much more difficult to heal a cancer than a wart; we think a million dollars is a lot of money and a dime isn't very much money; and we are right. But if we didn't know the one from the other and had never been told the difference, we shouldn't know. So the causation is right here.

I saw a cartoon one time of a Sunday School teacher asking the class about Daniel in the lions' den. The lions are there, like a bunch of kittens, very docile, and she asked the class, "Why didn't the lions attack Daniel?" Now, most of the kids answered that Daniel was taken care of by God; but one little kid said, "They were not afraid of him." She was the only one who had the right answer.

Have I told you about the young Episcopal clergyman who was told to take a shot of brandy? He was speaking for the first time, and his bishop was there. He finished and he rushed down, and the bishop said he did fine. He said, "You have the looks, you are young and handsome, your diction is perfect; but you haven't quite enough oomph. Even in our church you have to have a little pep. I will not object to your taking just a little glass of brandy before you go into the pulpit—for a little while, until you get warmed up to the situation."

The next week he had evidently followed the suggestion—and probably had not measured the glass very accurately: he was pretty pepped up! After the service, he came down to the bishop again and asked how he did. The bishop said, "You did wonderful; I *knew* it was in you. But I have to warn you about something: don't carry anything too far. Where you were telling the story about Daniel in the lions' den, you should have said, 'and by the grace of God, the lions were subdued.' You should not have said, 'and Daniel kicked the living hell out of them.'" You can see he entered into the spirit of it, anyway.

The Universe has the funniest way of putting the ridiculous and sublime together—else how can you account for our being here? It is impossible. There is an answer to this. Most people in our thought,* as in other religions, put on a long face and say, "Look at me and drop dead." Why is this? Because we seek to divide the indivisible. We

* = teaching.

arbitrarily place a limitation on everything we do. We think it is imposed on us by the Universe or by destiny.

Now, it isn't our fault! This is our bondage, our ignorance; this is our fall; and this is our sin—if we have one. But let us consider, next, that the entire Universe—all that God is, all that destiny may ever become, all that evolution shall ever produce—exists in its entirety at the standpoint of every manifestation within it, whether you and I call it big or little; good, bad, or indifferent; consequential or inconsequential—it doesn't matter. It doesn't know about these things. Remember, it doesn't know a mountain is bigger than a marble; it doesn't know our assumptions, else they would be true. Therefore infinity presses against the point of finiteness, and absoluteness against the point of relativity; and infinity is the finite. The finite is not the infinite, but the infinite is the finite.

Relativity is not absoluteness, absolutely; but absoluteness is relativity at the level of relativity, with nothing between the much and the more on the one hand, and what appears as the smaller and the lesser on the other. There are no mediators, Christs, saviors, avatars, Buddhas—all have to go by the wayside. They are no longer necessary to the evolution of the soul. How many know that they are *wayshowers* and not saviors? There is no such thing as a savior; don't ever tell anyone I said so, but it is true just the same.

It is a startling thing—Emerson said it is a cannonball. It is not always tender and gentle; it doesn't always appear even to be kind, because it is so impersonal.

Even having accepted its logic—which we must, if we think—we still do not quite catch its meaning, do we? Here, say, is a thing. The nature of its meaning may be explained; its essence can only be felt. Would that have any meaning? They have a saying in the theater about young actors and actresses—the director will say, "I didn't believe him. It wasn't real." "My words fly up, my thoughts remain below: words without thoughts, never to heaven go."

The logic of it is not difficult to understand; the mathematics of it is not difficult to understand: infinity undivided is omnipresent; and omnipresence is pressed against every point, flowing to that point in its entirety, and at that point existing only at that point, and for no other point. And that is the next thing I want to establish: individuation in the Universe. This is deep stuff for us to think about this summer.

How do we know this? Because no two thumbprints are alike; no two blades of grass are alike; no two snowflakes are alike; not any of you can jump in the same river twice; no moment coalesces, or combines, with any other moment. That is why Dean Inge said, "Time is a sequence of events in a unitary wholeness"; Augustine said, "It is anticipation, recollection, and memory." To more simplify these things, I just said, "Time is any measure of any experience but has no existence in and of itself. It is not an entity." The Zen Buddhist seeks to find that moment here, when *here* is no longer bound to *there* by a sequence of cause and effect. This is the reason why Jesus forgave people. He was right scientifically, logically, inspirationally, and in essence. *And it worked.*

To get back to the thought that, because of the uniqueness of every individual, it is necessary to say, "I hope it is; I would like to believe it is. Lead me to some prophet who will tell me, or some religion which will announce it, or some authority": there are no such things. "There are no prophets other than the wise." "The great are great to us only because we are on our knees; let us arise." The only greatness they have is that which we have loaned them from the inexhaustible magnitude of our own magnificence, as humble as we may be.

Emerson said, "There is a place in every man's life where the lines may run out full length." Genius is something that has not to be caught, but used; everyone has it. Now, it may be blocked by accident at birth. Physiologically, psychologically it may be blocked; but it still exists there, back of insanity, back of everything that looks crazy. It is why Browning said, "a god though in the germ." Well, we are screwy; but we are not crazy.

Genius—the possibility of everything, all that God is, all that the Universe has—exists solely that this rose shall bloom, that this man may paint this picture, that this girl may now go out and sing, that a child may make a mud cake and a mother nurse her baby—all of these. Isn't this a magnificent concept! The trivial is not incidental; it is merely the mode of manifestation of all things. The laughter of a child is as important to the Universe as the creation of a planet. A friend of mine* built the Golden Gate Bridge; it was the greatest engineering feat accomplished up until then, and possibly since then—I don't know —and the most difficult. He was the most childlike of persons.

A child builds a little house and kicks it over. The Golden Gate Bridge will someday fall down, rust out, be torn down, because something better will happen.

*Joseph Strauss (1870–1938), American bridge engineer.

Change is the only thing that is permanent. The only thing we can say of anything that looks static is: This too shall pass away. If it were not so, the Infinite would get caught in its own mold—God would be stopped by His own creation, and creativity would be absorbed in its creation.

I believe in pantheism to the extent that the soul of the Universe is in everything, but apart from it. That is why I said God is in His creation but not absorbed by it. This creation is necessary, and without it there would be no cause. It is impossible there should be a cause without creation. You would have an intelligence that is not intelligent of anything. A consciousness that is not aware of anything is not conscious—therefore it hasn't any existence; consequently it isn't and 't'ain't so. Therefore there is an infinite consciousness.

Now, this was what Bishop Berkeley* said—that "All things have to be in some mind." All things, he thought, were not in his intellect, therefore he supposed there is a Mind in which all things are real, but a Mind to which he has a relationship. Emerson said the same thing when he said, "Every man is an inlet to the same and to all of the same."

But now let's get back. We have the logic, we have the reason, we have the conviction; we believe these things, you and I, and perhaps most of the world does. They would if they understood them, I am sure. But to this intellectual concept, to this mathematical understanding, something else must be added. One is the Spirit, and the other the letter of the Law. A Universe without Law could

---

*George Berkeley (1685–1753), Irish philosopher. "To be is to be perceived."

never take form; a Universe without consciousness could never be creative. It is always a combination of the two: the thought and the feeling. Words, of themselves, are just words, are merely molds. There is no effective word without a meaning. You all have molds you use with your salads, etc.—you put something liquid in it and it takes form. But the mold is not the form of the *essence*.

There is, to the testimony of the intellect, the mind, the intelligence, the logic, and the reason, another and a higher testimony, which cannot be explained. For we may kill the nightingale and not capture the song; we may break an egg and not find the chicken. The mystery of life is just as much a mystery to God as it is to us, except God isn't *mystified* by it. I didn't used to know that.

There is no God which can explain God; if there were, then that thing we call *God* would be itself a secondary cause, subject to something beyond it. Therefore all inquiry into the Truth has to start where the Truth is. The thing *is* this way; life *is*. I live, therefore I am. You and I may just as well accept that infinity exists for the expression of everything, from a blade of grass to an archangel to a drop of water of the ocean.

The whole Universe is reflected in each speck of its own indivisibility, but the contemplation of that which permits the flow of its essence lies beyond the intellect and cannot be explained. It isn't beyond reason or rationality; it is beyond explanation and reasoning. Is that clear? We go through a process of reasoning to arrive at that which does not reason, but which if it did reason would always be reasonable. Jesus bore testimony to it in the same way when he said, "I judge no man; but if I judged, my judgment would be right." This is why Jesus, like the other great mystics, never explained anything. He said it is *like* this and *like* that—like grains of mustard seeds, and like whatever. That is why the poets never explained. It is an intuitive expression, a language that is beyond processes but which contains them.

Browning said, "All that is at all/ Lasts ever past recall." He doesn't go through an explanation and say life can't get dead, therefore it is going to live. He just says *that is the way it is.* They said to him, "What does it mean?" and he said, "I knew when I wrote it, but I don't know now." And that is true of all of us. Therefore there is a feeling; and there is an artistry. The art is mechanical; it is mathematical. Some warmth, some color, some feeling is breathed upon it through the artist by the original great Creativity; that thing about which Longfellow* in *The Song of Hiawatha* said: "He is gone, the sweet musician;/ He, the sweetest of all singers,/ Is gone from us forever./ He has gone a little nearer/ To the maker of all music,/ To the master of all singing."

So as we try to put these things together, the intellect is absolutely necessary: rationality, logic—all are necessary. But back of them all, and flowing through them all, there is something *beyond* them all—a feeling, an intuition. That is what religion is; that is what revelation is. That is why every great thinker who ever lived has told us that God does not argue; He contemplates. The barriers that we have to break down are the relativities— big and little, good and bad, right and wrong, Heaven and Hell. It is very difficult to do.

The experience of the race bears so much evidence that is negative, and it seems irrational to refute it. I do not

---

*Henry Wadsworth Longfellow (1807–1882), American poet.

know that we necessarily have to *refute,* as much as we have to *contemplate its opposite.* Without trying to bring opposites together, we will arrive at that viewpoint the poet must have had in mind when he said he viewed the world as one vast plane and one boundless reach of sky. Then would be brought to bear our simplest affirmation, the mandate of the Universe. If Lazarus hadn't come out when Jesus said, "Come forth," Jesus would have gone in and lain down with him.

We know that we are the offspring of Life, the manifestation of Light. We know that all the presence and all the power and all the love and all the wisdom and all the peace and joy and all the friendship and togetherness exist in this totality which we are, in which we embrace each other in love, in joy, and in peace. And it is our desire that there shall be unfolded to us—all of us—during this brief interval of our own contemplation a power so dynamic, a beauty so terrific, a peace so deep and a joy so flowing that Heaven and earth shall meet and make one vast music as before.

And so it is.

And God bless you.

CHAPTER 6

Money Is a Spiritual Idea

Ernest always had a high concept of an abundant Universe. In evening treatment (prayer work) in late 1958 and early 1959 he was cognizant of the need of money for the completion of Dr. Hornaday's church.* I always felt one shouldn't specify an amount as such, but rather pray for the need to be met. He believed differently and many times proved his consciousness by demonstrating the exact amount needed. To get me to understand his belief, he gave me three reprints from the magazine *The Uplift* of 1917 and 1918, which he had edited. They tell the story.

JESUS PAINTED THE tragedy of the unused talent. Natural gifts entail obligation to the giver. The greater the endowment, the greater is the responsibility. Every good and perfect gift cometh from God. We stand debtor to Him. We discharge the debt by using what He gives us. Among all those marvelous powers bestowed upon us by a gracious God, none stands higher than the faculty of thought. It is indeed supreme, for through it we employ every other faculty. Without it, all else is nothing. With

*Founder's Church of Religious Science.

it, even the meanest objects of nature are clothed in the uncounted wealth of things. Yet some people refuse to think! It is pitiful, tragic, incomprehensible. The thinker can but stand amazed before the thoughtless who contentedly mumble, "Ignorance is bliss." His astonishment increases when he stops to think that the thoughtless did not think out this thought. They accepted it. They were too indolent to challenge it, too lazy to think there was anything in it to challenge.

They follow in mental life the maxim of efficient industry, "Never do for yourself what you can get another to do." So someone else does their thinking. Not that they delegate anyone to do it—that would require thinking. They just let them do it. Like dried leaves in the current, they float into the channel that the winds and eddies of chance select. They accept what chance brings them.

In civic life, someone does their political thinking. They remain loyal to the party, even though they do not know its principle. In social life, they belong to their set. In professional life, they drift into a vocation. In religious life, they acknowledge the supreme authority of "the Church of their Fathers" and are unaware whether their religion is ancient enough to be "old time," or new enough to be "ragtime."

"Behold, the kingdom of God is within," and one who is to find it must look where it is to be found. "Speak to him, thou, for he hears,/ And Spirit with Spirit shall meet./ Closer is he than breathing,/ Nearer than hands and feet."

As we begin to get some grasp of this great indwelling power, we begin to see how it is that man is made but little lower than the angels. We begin to see that the first thing to do is to seek this inner kingdom, this spirit of God working through us, and we see how it is that from this seeking all else follows. This spirit is power, the only power, in the universe, the power of God. Can we imagine this power as ever falling short of its mark, as ever having to be told anything, as ever having to be helped to do anything? No, this is not *a* power; it is THE POWER, and we do well to let it guide and direct our way.

Not all the combined power and intelligence of the human race could produce a single rosebud, except it first comply with the Law. Money cannot buy this power, position cannot command it; it is not for trade.* And yet in the heart of the most humble as in the most exalted, this power forever dwells as the Spirit of the Most High. Is it, then, that as the Spirit of God dwells in man, it follows that he is God? No! As the child is not its father, so man is not God. He is in union with the Father. And as he more and more comes to realize this divine union of the Father and himself, he begins to see how it is that Jesus, who always lived from the spiritual standpoint, could say, "What the Son seeth the Father do, that doeth the Son also." Is this claiming too much from God? No! Are we not His image and likeness, and shall He not become glorified in us as we more and more put on this likeness and use it for the benefit of the world?

Let us, then, begin without fear to claim from the Spirit the things of the Spirit; this is the gift of the Infinite to His finite reflection, the gift of God to man. And as a gift, let us take it and make use of it. We must daily come to this

* = commerce.

indwelling Spirit to be made clean from our contact with the world. "Not by might nor by power, but by thy Spirit"* is our motto. Happy is the man who has found out this the greatest of all truths. Happy is he who dwells in this kingdom, and who draws from it his strength and his inspiration. He no longer listens to the voice of the world; he no longer becomes confused at the sight of outside appearances, for he knows that within is the power to change all and make all things work together for the good of all. Dwelling in the "secret place of the most High," he abides under the power of the Almighty. A peace that is more than all else comes to him and he is at home in the kingdom of God. "Then go not thou in search of him, / But to thyself repair; / Wait thou within the silence dim, / And thou shalt find him there." Peace comes from within.

THE RICH MENTALITY

With what vastness of power we may ally ourselves! What mighty energy is His who hurled the stars into ordered space! What infinite wisdom in their stately workings! What exquisiteness of beauty in the creative Mind that paints sunsets and adorns rainbows! What melody in His soul who teaches birds to sing! What depth of tenderness in Him who gave the mother-heart its love!

This energy, wisdom, beauty, and love—dynamic and creative—belong to the man whose simple, seamless fabric of faith is the deep abiding consciousness of the indwelling Presence, and who dares to draw forth the God

*See Zechariah 4:6.

97

within him. He shall have health, for he thinks it; wealth for he creates it; joy, for he gives it.

It is the simple, rich mentality of him who is in unity with the Spirit. Majestic is his power, satisfied is his soul, who, in the midst of the storm, despite the raging of men, in the chaos of material thinking, can enter into the silence and declare the absoluteness of his own being!

When we reach this high consciousness, we need only to speak the creative word, and it shall be done unto us even as we will. Herein is the secret of the perfect power of demonstration. The healer who can realize in his own consciousness the perfectness of being need do no more for his patient. Such consciousness is universal; and when it is true in his mind, it is true in all minds at all times and in all places. For God is present in His entirety at every point.

Nothing is more tragic than the blunders of the unthinking in any of these fields. Jesus was murdered because the mob didn't think and the leaders wouldn't. The history of the world, too, throngs with martyrdom of the great thinkers by petty ones. So Chrysostom* was expatriated and destroyed. Savonarola† was hanged, and Hus‡ was burned. Today, many men and women whose only offense is that they are thinking for the good of the people are being crucified by a mob of the unthinking, led by those who only half think—*their* half. They are martyrs to freedom of the press, honesty in government, and truth in religion.

*St. John Chrysostom (c.347–407), Church Father and patriarch of Constantinople.
†Girolamo Savonarola (1452–1498), Italian reformer.
‡Jan Hus (1372 or 1373–1415), Bohemian religious reformer.

My friends, the hardest thing in the world is to think, and the easiest thing in the world is to raise a hue and cry against the thinker. You have a mind, or at least God gave you one; is it your own or another's now? What governs YOUR actions? Do not answer "NEVER—MIND!"

MONEY A SPIRITUAL IDEA

Every time I talk on this subject I begin with this: I have no gold brick to sell. This is no get-rich-quick scheme. I have nothing at all to sell to you. There are no secret doctrines that will tell you how to make a million in a month.

While there is an exact science of gaining wealth, yet I will say, in beginning, that possibly none of you will ever prove it. Nevertheless, I will say that it is an exact LAW, a scientific and unfailing LAW. There IS a law of perfect supply.

To begin with, we must come to see that the supreme Intelligence must, in creating man, have also made a way by which he could be provided for in harmony and in peace and without robbing anyone of that which belongs to him. Now this way must be a natural way; it must be a natural law. Nature is always natural.

Now, we are talking about money, as that is the evidence of supply. Money is the highest medium of exchange that the race has as yet been able to produce. Jesus knew this, and he told his students to render unto Caesar the things that are Caesar's. He knew that money was an idea and a necessary one to the needs of human life. So there is a law of success, and all who will can prove it.

SUCCESS ISN'T DEPENDENT ON LOCATION

To begin with, does money depend upon location? Can it be made only in certain places? Let us see. In all places people make money; in all places there are some who are rich and some who are poor. Go to the smallest town, as well as to the largest city, and it is just the same—some are rich and some are poor. Success, then, does not depend on location.

Is it the kind of business? No. There may be two men in the same kind of business, equally well situated. One will make money, and frequently the other will lose. Does it depend on education? No. Some very ignorant men make money. Does it depend on a man's circumstances? On a man's bringing up? No. Some of the wealthiest men in the world began with nothing.

SUCCESS DEPENDS ON LAW

Upon what does it depend? It must depend on a certain, definite way of doing things. The man who succeeds must have succeeded through a certain method. The man who failed must have done entirely different. It must be a certain way of looking at it. There we get back into the spiritual realm.

There is a way which the Father hath provided by which we may demonstrate success. The way is there. I cannot go on the way for you; God cannot do that for you. You must walk the way yourself.

Now, as Browning said, "All's love, yet all's law." We are dealing with law—a mental and spiritual law. Now, law is not God; it is an attribute of God. So this law of success is not God, but it is an attribute of God. Man is given dominion over all laws, and when he comes to understand a law, he becomes the master of it. Jesus always referred to the Law and always complied with it. He so perfectly understood the Law that he could, with a word, make it work for him. Now the difference between Jesus and you and me is this: he could concentrate creation with his word. We do the same thing, only it takes us longer because of our unbelief. To illustrate: I once worked with a man who could add up several columns of figures at once and get a correct answer. I had to take the slower but nonetheless as-sure method of adding each column up separately. We both got the same answer, and we both did the same thing in getting it. One got it at once, the other got it by a slower method. Both were correct. One man can figure in his thought, the other has to use paper. But it is the same process.

We plant corn and let it grow, and then harvest it and make bread from it. Jesus said the word, and bread was made for him at once. Both methods are the same, in one respect, for both are natural. Now, then, what is this natural law that we can use? Is it something that we can come to understand and be sure of? Let us see if we can state it in simple and understandable words so that all may understand.

There is a mental atmosphere all around us; it is Mind and it is Intelligence; it knows, feels, hears, sees, and understands everything. It is universal—that is, it is ever present, it is always where we are. It is receptive—that is, it receives our thought; it has power to do anything, to produce anything, to create anything.

It is a great divine, natural medium and law. I am not going to try to convince you today that this Mind is a reality, for we have so often studied it. If you are spiritually developed enough, you will accept the fact and act upon it, and by so doing you will most surely reap the benefit of one who believes. If you cannot as yet accept the fact, you will be the loser. It matters not who takes it for a fact and who does not take it for a fact, the Law is there just the same. Happy is the man who can take it, for he shall reap the reward of the true son of his Father.

We ARE surrounded by this Mind, and we can use it just as we use any other natural law. You ask can we see, feel, hear, touch, taste or smell it? I answer "No." I ask about the law of gravitation: can you touch, taste, hear, see, feel, or smell it? You answer "No." We both must confess to a limited understanding of what the law really is, yet we both know that it exists. The things of the Spirit and Mind are not seen. The most sensible thing to do is to take all natural law for granted and instead of arguing over it, find out how to use it and how to reap the benefits of our knowledge.

We must have some faith if we are to live, so why not have a little more faith and live just that much more? Now, while this Mind is and works for all who will work it, to deal only with it as Mind is to deal only in mental law. This means limitation, and it is our endeavor to overcome limitation, and this can only be done through the Spirit. This mental law is an attribute of the Spirit, and we will get the best results only as we operate upon it in the Spirit. Jesus simply said, "Have faith in God." He knew that that would produce the required results.

But if a thing is true, there is a way in which it is true,

and this is the way: this Mind is there to be used; it is Mind—and the only instrument of Mind, the only tools of mind, are thoughts. Therefore we must look to thought to get our answer to the problem of success. The man who is a success is the man who, whether he knows it or not, is using natural law. I say "whether he knows it or not," for all are using this Law all of the time. Every time we think, we are "starting something," so to speak; that is, we are thinking into this Mind and it is doing the thing for us. Our word is our thought, so our word shall accomplish.

MAN NOT THE CREATOR

Now this word which we send out is going out into creative Mind. I say "creative Mind," for man does not create, he simply uses creation; and creative Mind is going to take it up and is going to bring back to us the thing that we have thought of. "I will send out my word and it will not return void." Now we are using Law, and Law is Mind in action, so we are putting Mind in action through the avenue of thought. Mental Law is thought going out to produce a certain definite result. The Bible says, "The Word [or thought] became flesh and dwelt among us": that is, the word or the thought became manifest to us. Thousands of people are today proving this to be true. Money, then, the same as all other things, is a spiritual idea.

CHAPTER 7

Religious Science and Man's Great Ideas

Dr. Holmes always, when he went to bed, read until he was tired. He wore a green plastic visor and would underline passages that impressed him. The last book he read before his transition was Aurobindo's *The Life Divine*. He suggested I should read it. I asked him how many pages it contained. When he told me it contained over 1,000 pages, I suggested that when he finished it he tell me about it. He didn't like that and shook his head sadly. In October of 1958, in a talk to a class of students, he emphasized reading as necessary for growth. This talk actually covered the relationship of humanity's great thoughts to Religious Science.

GOOD EVENING. I see I am surrounded by a great bunch of highbrows! We are embarked on an unknown voyage, which will be theoretical, speculative, mystical, and/or intuitive—which will be, or should be, logical and philosophical, and some of which is to be psychologically practical in applying what very little is known of the Principle of Mind to the persistent problems of life.

We happen to be a group of people who claim no infallibility whatsoever, and we never issue encyclicals or edicts. Those few of us here who have the privilege of talking to you happen to be here because we have the nerve to talk to you and you haven't any better sense than to listen to us. But that isn't *our* problem at all. So we should feel we are on pretty much of an equal basis, always remembering that the great are great to us only because we are on our knees. "There are no prophets but the wise."

There is no God in the Universe who ever tapped anybody on the shoulder and said, "I will deliver something to you that I have not given to anyone else." The last word will never be spoken, or God will pass out of existence.

So we happen to be in a certain place in the evolution of the human mind where we are able to stand up and look about us and survey our environment and recognize that, in a certain sense, we are separate and distinct from it; we are *other* than it. As the poet said, "A fire-mist and a planet, / A crystal and a cell, / A jellyfish and a saurian, / And caves where cave-men dwell; / Then a sense of law and beauty, / And a face turned from the clod— / Some call it Evolution, / And others call it God."*

I happen to believe we are all on the pathway of an endless evolution, that the impulsion back of the evolution is a divinely created spark which has impregnated us with "a Divinity that shapes our ends, rough-hew them how we will." I believe that every man is an incarnation of the one living Spirit; this one living Spirit is undivided and indivisible, and must, therefore, remain a total unit whose center is everywhere and whose circumference is

*William Herbert Carruth, "Each in His Own Tongue."

nowhere. At any and every point in it is infinity. Theoretically, there must exist all that it is, and not in fragments.

There is a certain process of reasoning that is called *axiomatic*, which means self-evident truths, things that the human mind could not deny. It is very apparent that we and all physical manifestation are in a process of some kind of evolution, from a lower to a higher form of life, of consciousness, of intelligence, and of awareness. It is equally self-evident that you cannot get out of a bag what is not in it; that which evolves must primarily, and first of all, have been *in*volved.

Have you read *Bible Mystery and Bible Meaning**? If you haven't, you should; it is a great book—the most intelligent book ever written on the Bible that I have ever read—one of the few books written on the Bible that I consider has very much intelligence. Most books on the Bible are just somebody's reaction to what they think the thing means. That is why we have so many different interpretations of it. They couldn't all be right—that is self-evident.

Now we are considering tonight the impact of the great thought of the ages upon our belief—our system of thought—which we happen to call Religous Science. Religious Science is not a revelation that I had. It is well that it is so—that we are this way and remain rational human beings, not overly influenced by anything nor coerced by our own desires until they project a false image of the self to appease the ego. We should be able, dispassionately but with feeling, to study the great thoughts of the ages.

*By Thomas Troward. It examines the Bible in the light of involution and evolution—i.e. in the light of the Law of Mind in action.

It is only through the great thinkers of the ages that we may learn what the human mind has discovered about its relationship to God. Neither will you find it in any one teaching, given by any one teacher or one system of religion or philosophy, nor will you find it comprehended in any one age.

I am reading three volumes on the writings of Hermes, who lived (it isn't definitely known whether he is a mythological person or not) 1500 years before Moses. I am reading practically everything that is of cosmic significance in our Bible and in the philosophy of Plotinus and Plato. You will find it in the Upanishads and the Vedas. You will find it in *The Book of the Dead* of the Egyptians; in the Bhagavad Gita. You will find it in every great religion that the world has ever had, and in every great system of thought, and in most of the great poets, and in all of the great mysteries and great mystery religions. We have to separate, somewhat, the wheat from the chaff.

Evelyn Underhill said, "The only news we have of the Kingdom of Heaven has come through the consciousness of man." We should swing between a contemplation of the mind and an action outwardly. I can only tell you what I believe, and you don't have to believe what I believe. We haven't got any set of beliefs or dogmas or anything like that. I believe something; you might believe something different. For instance, a number of our leaders believe in reincarnation, and to me it is ridiculous; but I won't argue with them.

I discovered a long time ago: life would be very simple if everyone would agree with me. But I also discovered that they didn't. So I said, "Well, let's let everybody believe what he wants to. If what he believes is true, we can't help it; if what he believes is not true, it can't hurt anything." I think it's important to maintain a good-natured flexibility in all our studies, to realize that no matter how much we study each day's accumulation of knowledge and facts, be they physical, psychic, or spiritual, they but give us a fresh starting point for something else. "Ever as the spiral grew,/ He left the old house for the new." I believe things today that would have scared me to death 30 years ago if I had ever thought about them or that they might be true. You will find the same experience.

As knowledge increases and contemplation broadens its base that it may deepen its perspective, it will at the same time heighten the apex of its receptivity. Values will change. While living in the same Universe, we will discover that we are living in a different one, but that it is attached to the same one.

We have to look to the great thoughts of the ages to discover what the world has found out is true. If we look to only one of the great thinkers—there are no exceptions to this—we will not discover as much truth as we would if we looked to all of them. When we look to all of them, unless we have a good ability to synthesize, we might very easily become confused. It is a very difficult problem and proposition to have liberality of mind and not to read everyone's thought. I do it continuously. I have a half-dozen books I am reading all the time. I pick them up and read them so I won't get caught too much in any one and get shifted onto a different track. (It just happens to be my method.) I find what Lowell called "that thread of the all-sustaining beauty that runs through all and doth all unite."

In my own mind, I am more teachable and more flexible today than I was 40 years ago. At that time, being new, young, crude, and raw, I thought I knew it all. Someone said, "I used to think I knew I knew,/ But now I must confess/ The more I know I know,/ I know I know the less."

Count Keyserling,* who taught 30 or 35 years ago, would not take anyone in his classes until they had reached the age of 40. He said they were too immature; they hadn't developed the ability to think. And now they don't let people take professions after they are 40 for fear they are too old. How strange and inconsistent! We have to turn to the thoughts of the ages and analyze them one by one; then, as we analyze, we must synthesize, or put together.

Now, if you read *Cosmic Consciousness* by Bucke (and if you haven't, you will),† you will find a man who had a very deep knowledge of the difference between spiritual illumination and psychic hallucination. He cites about 60 cases, as I remember, of those who undoubtedly have had illumination or been cosmically illumined. They had a deeper perspective, understanding, appreciation of, feeling toward, and knowledge of the spiritual nature of man and of reality. He shows, by an analysis, certain fundamental things that they all believed in and that we are justified in accepting.

These are things that do not contradict each other, if, indeed, we are justified at all—which I believe we are—in

*Hermann Alexander Keyserling (1880-1946), German social philosopher whose philosophy centered on the theme of spiritual regeneration.
†Richard Maurice Bucke (1837-1902), Canadian psychoanalyst and author.

believing that the human mind has revealed anything. We have no source to go to other than the sources which we call *human*—no matter how divine they may have been. These are the only sources; we have no other knowledge of reality.

Bucke showed a half-dozen main things, including a consistent belief in immortality; a consciousness of the absolute unity of all things; a realization that everything is in a process of evolution; and a consciousness that there is no fundamental, basic, essential entity of evil in the Universe. Now, that was his synthesis after carefully analyzing—with the ability to analyze the difference between psychic hallucination and spiritual realization and cosmic illumination. He found certain persistent facts running through the lives of these outstanding persons from all walks of life, facts which we may accept as valid and real. We have every reason to believe that it is so.

We have to look to the spiritual realization of the ages to discover this spiritual truth, whether it is in Jesus or Buddha; or the philosophic, whether it is in Emerson or Plato. We have to look to scientific research. In our system, we believe that the Universe is one system, and *but* one. Every apparent part and every apparent segment of it reveals the nature of all of its other parts—*all* of them. For instance, attraction and repulsion, demonstrated in physics and the Universe, is one system. We should expect to find the same attraction, repulsion, adhesion, cohesion, and polarity in the mind: the Universe is fundamentally a thing of intelligence. As Emerson said, "The mind that wrote history is the mind that reads it." Human history is a record of the doings of that Mind on this planet.

We start with the supposition *God is all there is*—all life, truth, reality. Life, God, Spirit, or Reality is incarnated in each one of us, equally and evenly distributed to all. As Jesus said, "He causes his sun and rain to come alike on the just and on the unjust."

We have to start with the proposition, then, that there is that in me which can understand what anyone has ever said or known or taught or done. I shall be interpreting the action and reaction of that which is identical with myself, in myself, for which I have an affinity. Kant said, "We are able to recognize an apparently external object because it awakens an intuition within us in a field of common denominators." That sounds awesome and gruesome; that is the way these guys talk. All he meant was this: I look up here and see the mountain. I didn't put the mountain there, but I can recognize the mountain, because the Mind that put the mountain there is the Mind that put me here.

"There is one mind," as Emerson said, "common to all individual men." Therefore it awakens an intuition or a perception—I know you only because the Mind which you are and the Mind which I am is recognizing itself in each other. That is the discovery Lowell made or caused to be made in *The Vision of Sir Launfal*, that finally comes out, "I behold in thee the image of him who dies on the tree."

Now, people in our field are always trying, or should be, to develop their consciousness—to expand, deepen, and broaden and heighten their awareness of life. For instance, I happen to be reading for the third time one of the most remarkable books I have ever read. The man believed in reincarnation; he spends about a hundred pages out of 900 explaining why it is so. I haven't the slightest idea it *is* so, but he had. Outside of that, we get along beautifully. Maybe he is right and I am wrong. If he is right, I can't help it; if I am right, he can't help it.

We may *believe* what is, is not so; we can only *know* what *is* so. Knowledge is of reality; belief is of theoretical supposition, which may or may not be true. That is what is the matter with a great deal of our philosophy: it gets nowhere because it starts nowhere. Its premise being wrong (although its logic may be perfect), its conclusion will be completely in error.

The other night, I read a statement in *The Life Divine* —one of the great books of modern times; you must read it; Gandhi and Tagore considered Aurobindo the greatest spiritually enlightened intellect of modern India, so you know he must have been somebody; he only passed on a few years ago. He said that the transcendence, by which he means the Absolute (we would call it the Reality, the Finality, God, or Truth), does not *reconcile*; it *transmutes*. I said to myself, "This is one of the greatest things I have ever heard." Now, I have read it several times before, several years ago. Then I loaned the book to Barclay Johnson and he read the same thing and was struck by it. *The transcendence does not reconcile—it transmutes.* I said to myself, "This is a great saying," and I laid the book down (I do all my reading after I go to bed), and I said, Just what does the guy mean? And so I thought for about a half-hour before I went on. Then I put it in my own words.

I find myself in reading the great thoughts. We should continually read them. It is like talking to a great mind, holding conversation with a heavenly guest. It is terrific. It is something we can't afford to be without—just as we cannot afford not to be surrounded by beauty. No one can afford to be without love, beauty, happiness, and action. Love is the only protection and the only security there is in the Universe. Beauty unveils the invisible to us. Action is the only thing that releases the tension of the accumulated emotions (psychologically) and realizations (spiritually) that seem to be pressing against everything. When it does not move into the explosion of self-expression spontaneously, it is repressed into the unconscious, and this is the cause back of all neurosis—not some of it, but *all* of it.

I thought, Now what is Aurobindo saying? What does he mean when he says this? I always try to find out: What does this person mean? If it seems a little involved, I put the book down and make up my mind what the fellow meant when he said it. I think of everything that is related to it that comes to my mind and synthesize it with what other people have said. It just flows through my mind like this, rather quickly; because if I have ever made any contribution, this is it. I am not an original thinker—but it *is* original to know you are not.

I say in my own language, to myself, "This is what he meant; this is what it means to me." I have transformed a language with which I am not familiar into a terminology which I understand because it is my own. Have you ever tried that? You will be surprised how it helps to hold a thing in consciousness. So I said, "Now, this is a great saying." Then I thought: the Bible said, "Be still, and know that I am God." Lao-tzu* said, "All things are possible to him who can perfectly practice inaction." Long

*6th century B.C. Chinese philosopher; traditionally, author of *Tao-te Ching*.

since, I came to know the only thing in the Universe that cannot be resisted is nonresistance; and as one after the other of sayings of great people with whom I was familiar came to my mind to coincide with this, I said, "Now what does it mean to me?"

I no longer cared what it meant to Plato or Socrates or Aristotle or Jesus—because they came and they went, even as words written on the sands of time, to be blown away by the wind. Nothing is permanent but your self; nothing is unshakable. I said in something I wrote, "Hid within all things evolved/ In silence: beauty, wisdom, will,/ Is that which makes the cycle move:/ Unmoved, immovable, and still." It was inspired by reading the Gita, so it isn't entirely original, but a way of saying that at the center of every person there is that which doesn't move, and everything moves around it. That is you—that is myself—a unique representation of the infinite and ineffable One and Only, beside which there is none other.

I said to myself, "The transcendence does not reconcile"; and I remembered Jesus said, "You cannot serve God and mammon. . . . Judge not according to appearances but judge righteously." And I remembered that the Gita said, "You cannot enter into bliss while you deal with pairs of opposites." Do you begin to see what it means? *The transcendence transmutes*—it does not reconcile opposites; they clash. And I said, "This is what it means to me: the rays of the sun will melt an iceberg, even two icebergs floating side by side that could easily crush the Empire State Building should they clash from both sides of it." Emerson said, "The physical universe is spirit reduced to its thinness, oh so thin." This is what great reading will do for you: it brings to you the wisdom

of the ages. Automatically, your own consciousness coor-
dinates, synthesizes, as the intellect analyzes. Something
inside of you synthesizes, and you never forget it.

Emerson also said, "We see the universe as a solid fact,
God sees it as liquid law." And then I thought: Quimby
said, "Mind is matter in solution; matter is mind in form."
His dual unity of one whatever-it-may-be is as the matter of a superior wisdom which governs it.* I thought
about what Plotinus said: "If I were to impersonate the
Infinite, God, I would say, 'I do not argue; I do not contend; I contemplate. And as I contemplate, the images of
my thought form into what is called this great indetermi-
nation of nature, which is more than nothing and less
than something, having no mind of its own, but being
moved upon by that which is a superior thing to it." And
I said, "All right!"

Now, then: that is what it means to me philosophically.
I got very elated and lit up. Now I said to myself, "This
is what it means philosophically; it is right. If the Universe
is one system, there is a transcendence which governs
everything, there is an Intelligence which controls everything, since it is One-and-Only-and-All and has not an
adversary." "I will contend with him that contendeth with
thee, saith the Lord." And that flashed through. You see
how things come together? I said, "What does it mean in
practice? *You have no adversary; you have no enemy;
you have in that transcendence nothing to heal as though
it were an entity, or change as though it were a confusion.
You* do *have practicality.*"

*I.e. to which it is plastic. For a reliable and brief exposition of
Quimby's thought, see Ervin Seale, *Mingling Minds* (DeVorss).

You are not dealing with a pair of opposites, or good or evil, or God or mammon; we have been warned by all the great thinkers not to—and now I know why. I only wish that my heart knew what my intellect proclaimed in those 30 minutes; but it doesn't, because it still gets sad, because we are human. We just get to look through the veil temporarily, as some great mind lifts the veil from before the face of Isis; we see the form, the beauty, the warmth, and the color of that which is a part of Reality, closer to us perhaps than our very breath. The Talmud says, "nearer to us than our neck vein."

It is something, as one of the great poets said, "To see clear-eyed the future as we see the past,/ From doubt and fear and hope's illusion free"—said Sill.* (I didn't know, when I started to say it, who wrote it). "To see clear-eyed the future as we see the past,/ From doubt and fear and hope's illusion free": first time I ever knew of hope being referred to as an illusion—and it is an illusion.† It is an illusion to a greater thing; it is transcendent of a lesser one. It is a salutary attitude, but there is one beyond it, which is one of certainty.

I said, "What does this mean to me?" It means that in treatment, if I can get my mind still, "Look unto me, and be ye saved, all the ends of the earth." Look to the One-Only. Plotinus said our work is done better when our face is turned toward the One, even though our back is turned to our work.

That is no different from saying, "Be still, and know

*The reference may be to Milton Sills, co-author, with Holmes, of *Values* (1932).
†He himself refers to it thus in *The Science of Mind* ("Hope a Subtle Illusion"), p. 49.

that I am God"; "Look unto me, and be ye saved, all the ends of the earth." So I said, "Here is a transcendence that does not deal with opposites; therefore it doesn't resist, and consequently it conquers them." "And the light shines in the darkness, and the darkness comprehendeth it not." And so forever more it is set in my mind and it will never leave it. It will never leave me. I took 30 minutes, maybe an hour, just to think about this one thought: the *transcendence does not reconcile—it transmutes.*

And I likened it even to what is called sublimation in psychology, which is defined as deflecting the energy of the Id into socially useful purposes. Now, if I say, "sublimation is a deflecting of the energy of the Id into socially useful purposes," I am saying exactly the same thing— but there aren't any psychologists who would know you were saying the same thing. What they mean is this: if the neurosis is resolved, it is not resolved by bringing another contention with which to combat it, but by actually translating, transmuting. They call it sublimation: deflecting, transmuting, a lower form of energy into a higher, without contention. That is the exact meaning of pyschological sublimation. In our language we would call it *transmutation.* It is the meaning of the alchemist: to transmute a lower or base metal into pure gold or a higher one. (But they have back of it symbolism.)

Remember, this external act and endeavor of the alchemist was stimulated by the intuition of an inner knowing, beyond processes of reasoning, that everything in the Universe is made of one stuff. While every separate thing has its formula, if the formula is changed, the form will translate itself into something else—and it takes so little to change it.

This is what great reading does for us. It does another thing, in my estimation, which is psychological, or psychic, or subjective. I believe it puts our consciousness in rapport with the consciousness of the writer—not necessarily where he now is, but in the state of consciousness that he was in when he was here. Maybe it goes beyond this—I am not arguing about that; I do not know. In this way, we read between the lines. This is why we read great poetry. This is why, when you read thoughts, always you are getting something that "wasn't there before"; but it *was* always there.

I definitely believe that these thoughts exist in the Universe. I think they are indestructible. And I believe we get in vibration or rapport with them. This is what happens in psychism; (this is known and scientifically demonstrated). Now why, then, should it not follow: if we go the whole limit, we should enter into thoughts of others beyond anything they expressed—while what they expressed was merely like a more objective psychometric reading.

By holding a physical object, you are contemplating a thought that someone had: it doesn't seem strange to me that that should happen in psychometry. They will take the physical object, like this watch, and you know what happens: they enter into the subjective state of it—another dimension of it; but it is real. It is a terrific illusion and delusion, but the thing is real. We must not be afraid to play with things merely because there is a certain danger. Emerson said he had no patience with a man who, having read that somebody committed suicide by cutting his throat with a razor, would never use a razor again.

I told Barclay* the other day, "I have coined a new expression for what we are; and if somebody asks me now what we are, I am going to say: we are practical idealists and transcendental realists." I think that is good. Because, in order to be ideal we are not going to desert the real; in order to be transcendental we are not going to desert what is so. We do not say we are trying to heal people of what does not ail them. That is ridiculous.† I have noticed that people who do this are very liable to fall into the error of coercing their own consciousness until finally they are running around denying everything they don't like and affirming everything they do. That is a very great danger. "Keep faith with reason, for she will convert thy soul." "There are no prophets but the wise."

I believe it brings a psychological or psychic as well as a spiritually illumined state of consciousness. We cannot afford not to read people like Emerson, Plato, Jesus, Buddha, Socrates, Mary Baker Eddy; I love them, and they are all great people; and truth belongs to no one. If it was their great privilege to reveal something beyond the ordinary, still, that which they revealed belongs to the ordinary. Jesus said, "I came that ye might have life and that ye might have it more abundantly," and when they confused him with the life he came to reveal he said, "It is expedient that I go away that the Spirit of truth shall bear witness—that you shall awake within yourself." As Paul said, "Awake thou that sleepest, and arise from the dead, and Christ shall give thee light."

Now, we may start out with the proposition that we

---

*Barclay Johnson.
†I.e., we do not deny their experience of an ailment.

can learn only from the great; but all science, all knowledge is built up a little here and a little there. We are beneficiaries of the ages. Truth belongs to no one, no group of people, no class of people—never did and never will. You and I too, fortunately—if we *are* so fortunate —might add something not to the sum total of truth itself, but to the sum total of the accumulating knowledge that men have.

I always like to ask a practitioner, when I see he or she has done some outstanding thing or work, "How did you feel inside yourself when you treated this person?" I don't care what words they said. "My words fly up, my thoughts remain below:/ Words without thoughts, never to heaven go." Jesus could stand in front of Lazarus and tell him to get up and come out. If I were having a funeral and I told the corpse to arise and the corpse got out of the casket, the people would jump right through the wall.

We are four-dimensional people living in a three-dimensional world. But there ever more are echoes from beyond the shores of time which are singing of the timeless. There are always impingements upon our intuition and even our physical being, I believe; a gentle urging and pushing. "There is a spirit in man," Job said, "and the inspiration of the Almighty giveth them understanding." Jesus said, "The wind bloweth where it listeth, and thou . . . canst not tell whence it cometh, and whither it goeth: and so is everyone who is born of the Spirit." "God is Spirit and seeketh such."

Emerson said, "We should set up a lowly listening." We are also told to beware, to be careful that this listening is done with intelligence. I would rather speak ten words with my understanding than a thousand without it. It is a very fine thing to think straight, but we have the guidance of the greatest thinkers of the ages. We have scientific research, if we can put it together with psychology and metaphysics, which will spell to us the synthesis of an animating principle that repeats the same thoughts over and over and over again.

The Hermetic teaching said, "What is true on one plane is true on all: as above, so beneath." Which merely means this: physical, spiritual, and mental laws coincide. They are the same laws. They are not three sets of different laws: they are but one set of laws functioning on different levels, be it physical, mental, or spiritual. That is why we say, "We translate the physical symbol into its metaphysical meaning." Start out with that, and it would change the nature of the physical. There is no one thing that we can do that is more valuable to us than repeatedly to read the thoughts of great people. The thoughts of the great people remind us—and the lives of great men all remind us—that "We can make our lives sublime, / And, departing, leave behind us / Footprints on the sands of time, / Footprints that perhaps another, / Walking o'er life's solemn main, / A forlorn and friendless brother, / Seeing, may take heart again"—Longfellow.

We "never forget"—but we don't always remember! True, isn't it? Then, from these thoughts we are led to formulate our own thinking. Great thoughts induce in us a chain of thinking—a sequence of thinking that stimulates our own consciousness not only to a new endeavor, but also to the discovery of new pathways; they open up a new possibility for the expansion of our own minds. That is probably the greatest thing that they do; nothing that comes to us can do anything more than awaken an intuition on the level of that which comes to us. Is that clear? It was already there potentially; this drags it out. We couldn't perceive it if it weren't there so we could see it; but it does stimulate that greater possibility—it bores a hole down, as it were, in our own consciousness and lets up a new gusher, a new freedom, a new expansion. We cannot afford not to companion with the great and the good and the wise of the ages. Now, this takes time—but it is worthy of our effort. It takes thought and thinking and is the most difficult task on earth. It takes analysis and synthesis, which calls for bringing intelligence to bear, that we may discover that which we have inherited from the ages. That is the legacy of every sane and intelligent person. As Emerson said, "Only a few people in each age can understand, or do understand, Plato—but to every age the works of Plato are brought and placed in the hands of these few as though God himself had brought it."

There is a natural affinity of thought, since like attracts like and birds of a feather flock together. I believe that as we companion with the great thoughts of the ages, we draw not only from the great thinkers we might be perusing now, but from other thoughts that more or less are in harmony with them. There is, it seems to me, in the psychic storehouse of our world the accumulated knowledge of the ages. Now the occult has called this the Akashic records; if you ever heard of it, that is what it means. I think Jung calls it *the collective unconscious*, and I think that is true enough.

We shall keep it very simple and say: there is a repository of all the thoughts of the ages. Just as you and I have a memory, some little incident will bring things to mind, just like the verse I just read—I had forgotten who wrote it or where it was from.* There is a world mind and memory which Jung was the first one to speak of as the individual and collective unconscious—and we all draw upon it. It is a source of much inspiration because there is somewhere, if we can get a handle on it, this accumulated knowledge that flows through every instrumentality that is more or less open to it.

Stimulating our own thoughts is like an exercise. We should not just skim over the pages lightly and say, "What a great guy!" Take time to let the meaning sink deep until, finally, whatever it means to that man, it now means to you. We have captured his wit, his will, and his imagination and made it our own. We don't do it by stealing it from him, but because here it is, and it belongs to everyone. And more and more we shall find our reading expands our consciousness—if we contemplate its meaning; if we think about it.

Great thoughts begin to awaken in us, and you will be surprised how right Emerson was when he said, "Sometimes the muse too strong for the bard sits astride his neck and writes through his hand." Every man may write beyond his intellectual comprehension; every man may speak, at times, a language the meaning of which he does not comprehend. I am not talking about psychic confusion—I am talking about something beyond that. Every man is a revelator of the whole thing.

That is why Emerson said, "Watch that spark that flashes across your own consciousness; it is the one and only solid fact that you possess." It is all that you brought with you; it is a cinch it is all you will ever take away

*See p. 116.

with you. This is a pearl of great price, for which a man will sell all that he has in order that he may possess it, the wonder of it, the beauty of it, and the thrill. (You know there is a little ham in every preacher or nobody would come to listen to him. I am willing to admit it; and if I haven't got it, I would like to have it!)

Every man may speak, think, act, and write beyond his own comprehension. If he doesn't do it and think beyond the day of yesterday, tomorrow will find the old monotonous pattern, as Freud* said, repeating itself over and over again and playing its tune over and over and over again. We live under the hypnosis of the ages. Try to originate thought out of this greatness; feel yourself to be unique and great without being conceited. It isn't any of your business that God Almighty put his spirit into your soul and animated your being with His life; it is none of your business, and don't *let* it be any of your business. You must not confuse this with the little peewee who occasionally wakes up, squeaks, and soon sinks back into the slumber from which he had only become half awake.

Very deep in you and in me is the source, the reason, the essential cause, the destiny, the evolution, Heaven and Hell, God, man, and the Devil, the possibility of all things—if we will listen simply, sincerely, almost impersonally. Never confuse the little we know with the much that might be gathered as by a child joyfully, enthusiastically clapping its hands. This is why Jesus said, "Verily I say unto you, their angels do always behold the face of my Father which is in heaven."

*Sigmund Freud (1856–1939), Austrian neurologist and founder of psychoanalysis.

CHAPTER 8

Our Mission to the World

Ernest always felt that the strength of Religious Science was in the member churches. He had great personal interest in all the ministers; one in particular was Dr. John Hefferlin* from Long Beach. Ernest had shared with me that people at national headquarters didn't think that John should be a minister. But Ernest recognized something in him and overruled them. He always said that you can teach ministers comparative religion, the Bible, and many things, but until you put them in a pulpit, you would never know.

On the evening of January 8, 1959, at a church banquet concluding a week-long meeting of representatives and ministers from all the churches, he expressed his feeling to the people. He was introduced following a talk of acceptance from Dr. Hefferlin, and it was fitting that the last lines of John's talk reflected Dr. Holmes' continuing beliefs. It emphasized Ernest Holmes' great humility, as you can sense from Donald Curtis't introduction, which followed.

---

*(1903–1987), Religious Science minister.
†At the time, Religious Science minister.

JOHN HEFFERLIN (last part of his speech)

We have learned the power of imagination, but there is one other power. We may have all the treatment in the world, we may have all the feeling, all the imagination, but I tell you this one thing: without a spiritual awakening, without a spiritual awareness beyond the imagination and beyond the intellect, we will remain as grasshoppers. But with the awakened soul, with the awakening of the spirit within us, we too become giants, not only of the present, but on into the future of mankind. Thank you and God bless you.

DONALD CURTIS

Tonight, in line with the request of our beloved dean, founder, and leader—Dr. Holmes—as he comes to the podium to speak, he has asked that you do not rise, and I would suggest we tender him that great tribute too of perhaps withholding our applause, because this might well be the greatest applause of all—because we know this will be the climax in consciousness and guidance for us to sustain this spiritual refilling throughout the year to come.

I wish all of you here at the banquet could have been at the opening session of the convention this year when Dr. Holmes spoke. But we have possibly, if it *were* possible, even a greater treat in store now. I can't help but compare the level of consciousness in Dr. Holmes to the modern parable which is told of the old minister and the new minister.

There was a testimonial dinner given for a founding minister in a church. He had over the years turned out a great many great people, leaders in society, in the ministry. They sent for the most famous of them, a man who had made his mark as a great orator; he was known throughout the world. They brought him to give the testimonial speech, and he talked on the 23rd Psalm. He expounded, he explained, and he sat down after reciting it, and the applause was deafening. Then the beloved founder got up, and he simply recited the 23rd Psalm. There was no mistaking the silence and the depth of the response.

As he was traveling back to the airport, the great man, known throughout the world, was a little chagrined and piqued. He asked his companion, "Didn't I give a good talk? What was wrong with my rendition of the 23rd Psalm?" His friend said, "Well, it was this way: you knew the 23rd Psalm; but the old minister, our founder—he knows the Good Shepherd." Ladies and gentlemen, Dr. Holmes.

ERNEST HOLMES

THANK YOU, DON; it was very sweet and very deeply appreciated.

I would like to explain the real reason why I asked that you didn't stand up. It is that it isn't a good habit before the world. I love it and appreciate it passionately; but we have a principle that we practice, and we teach something that is the common denominator of every man, and it is only because of your great generosity, and my liking it so much, that we kind of formed this habit. I do appreciate it—have always—but we have overdone it, I think, and you will understand that. I love it. I would like to take each one of you in my lap and rock you to sleep. But instead of that, I will have to try to wake you up, I guess.

But you know, in the eyes of the world, who know not very much about Religious Science, we are a small group compared to the population of this city or the world. It might give a false impression. We do not deny or decry the personality of man; it is the only evidence we have of his divinity. But we do proclaim that inward Man, which is the common denominator of all human beings. In my belief, one man is neither better nor worse than another man. In my belief, every person is on the pathway of an eternal evolution.

I hold with the ancient Hindu teaching of the divine incarnation, from which the Christian concept of theology came in very inadequate form and was surrounded by superstition and ignorance. Until now the central flame has practically died out in the consciousness and in the awareness of those who would interpret the meaning of the incarnation. For all men are divine or no men are divine; every man is an incarnation of God or no man is; every man is immortal or no man is immortal.

There is nothing good enough that you and I can do to earn the privilege to live, and there is nothing evil enough we can do to destroy it. Browning said, "Fool! All that is, at all,/ Lasts forever, past recall;/ Earth changes, but thy soul and God stand sure:/ What entered into thee/ That was, is, and shall be:/ Time's wheel runs back or stops: Potter and clay endure."

We have the most wonderful time together. I have never seen in so large a body of people so much love, so much affection, so much understanding. There has been no discordant note, no criticism—it has been almost beyond belief, the experience we have all passed through these last four days. I shall never forget it. It is an experience that can come only from a group of people who are happily, normally, and sanely dedicated to an idea, without walking around thinking they look like a bunch of saints, which I would detest. We have no saints, we have no saviors, we have no prophets, we have no priests. We have a very deep simplicity in our philosophy, a very simple approach to reality. It is as profound as Plato, and I have studied Plato all my life—although I don't claim to understand him. There is no philosophy that has ever been given to the world more profound than ours, nor has one ever been given that is more simple.

I have naturally been gratified that John Hefferlin and his wonderful church have united with us.* He is like a son to me, and Mrs. Hefferlin is like a daughter and a very beautiful one, don't you think? And I am so happy Don Curtis is with us on our board and is a representative from John Hefferlin's church. Last year, Fred Bailes† came to me and said he would like to find someone to take over his very great and flourishing church, and that there would be no other organization in the entire New

---

*In 1954, 19 member organizations (churches) of a total of approximately 65 enrolled in the International Association of Religious Science Churches declined to enter into the new organizational arrangements proposed by the Institute of Religious Science. The 19 included Hefferlin and his Long Beach church. In December 1958 Hefferlin, who had found Holmes "very shocked and grieved" by the split, returned with his church to the Institute (now the United Church of Religious Science). See Marian Hefferlin, *A Time to Remember* (Los Angeles, 1991), pp. 261–63, 270–71, 279.

†(1889–1970), minister and teacher of the Science of Mind and sometime collaborator with Ernest Holmes.

Thought or metaphysical movement from which he felt he could choose a leader other than ours. That is a great tribute to us.* However, it is true—like the little boy whose mother said, "You think you are pretty good don't you?" and he said, "No, mother, I don't think I am good at all, because I know I am a lot better than I think I am." Now, we are better than we know—very much better, indeed.

The keynote of our convention has been *togetherness* —the unity of our thought and purpose and plan and action for the extension of our work and for the deepening of our own consciousness in that field of divinity "that shapes our ends, rough-hew them how we will." I have never felt so much affection, personally and collectively —and it is the greatest thing in the world. I have learned in the last year and a half† that no one does anything for himself—it is absolutely impossible. *We live unto others.*

Now that isn't just a sweet saying. We live unto others because that which is myself is yourself; that which is yourself is myself; that which is ourself collectively and ourselves individually is the one and only self there is— there is no other self. I believe we are living in a spiritual Universe right now, surrounded by perfect situations, by perfect people, and by perfect events. Such intellectual training as I have, any such capacity of reasoning or rationality I might possess, would deliver that to me axiomatically: it is self-evident.

*Donald Curtis became Bailes' successor upon the latter's retirement in 1959.
†This coincides with the period following his wife's death in May 1957.

The intellect can arrive at an intelligent profundity which is far beyond our inward understanding and our embodiment. God is all there is; there isn't anything else —there never was and never will be. Even that which appears not to be God is God in disguise. As Emerson said, "We are on a drunk that seems as though somebody or something gave us something too strong to drink when we entered this world and we are in a perpetual sleep; but once in a while someone wakes up." Now, we are trying to wake up to something within us and something cryptic, hidden in the Universe, always ready to be revealed.

I believe the divine pattern of perfection—not a plan, but a pattern—is resident in everything. That energy, force, intelligence, will, consciousness, desire, feeling— call it what you will—that came with the early dawn contained within it the pattern not only of perfection but of the whole evolution of man; and everything that has happened in evolution is but the unfoldment of that pattern through the thought, feeling, intellect and action of man. That pattern contains what is beyond our present perception. This is the secret that Jesus had.

This is what Buddha discovered when he found out what the Psalmist meant when he said, "Thou hast led captivity captive." He was called the Man of the Heart.* We belong to the Christian philosophy; we are a Christian denomination;† it is what we mean by the Christ. Christ does not mean Jesus; Jesus embodied the Christ. It is what the Buddhists mean by the "Enlightened One," what the Hindus mean by Atman, or the universal and divine incarnation of the Absolute.

*Refers to the divine Ideal and not to the Buddha. See p. 133.
†But see vol. 2, *The Anatomy of Healing Prayer*, p. 184.

There is, in you and in me, a unique presentation of this—that by the very nature of the process of our evolution we should finally spring full-orbed into our divine nature and consciously cooperate with it. There is that which must wait until slumber passes from our eyes and the inertia from our minds; the Spirit within us proclaims it to us. I do not believe that we as individuals or the race evolve spiritually, other than through our own consent—otherwise we would not be individuals. But if that is true, then there is that within us that we should get together with.

Now, we have been talking about getting together organizationally. It is all necessary—personally, that is all necessary. We love each other; and I trust it shall be increasingly said that this is a group of people who love each other—who are at least making a bold effort to turn every negation into an affirmation, every denial into an acceptance, every no into a yes, every evil into a good, every lack, every want, into an abundance.

The Universe imposes nothing on us but a freedom so great that we tie the cords of that freedom around us in our ignorance and believe that *they* are imposed upon us. There is nothing in the Universe that can will us other than freedom. The Universe has a certain nature; God has a certain nature; and we shall spring forth full-orbed. We shall come into the divine inheritance of that which the Infinite has bequeathed to us only on its own terms—not on ours. We shall not do it in exclusion; we shall not do it in hate; we shall not do it through unloveliness. There is something poetic about it.

You see, everything in the Universe springs from an absolute silence equally distributed everywhere, and this so moves that everything in movement will contain number and color and tone. We shall not do it, then—as John has said, and rightly so—just through the intellect.* We need the intellect, God knows, and we could use a lot more of it than we have; but there is another Man inside us that we shall have to get together with. I think this is a secret we all share with God; it is a secret we share with ourselves; and I have of late years become increasingly aware of this whatever-it-may-be, call it what you will.

As Wordsworth said, "The experience we have with it in the silence of our own soul is still, be it what it may, the light of all our day." And it is not an illusion; it is not a hallucination. There is that which is within us which is first cause and the only cause and the last cause and the present cause and the active cause. Now, very few people understand the philosophy of metaphysics. As I explained this morning, we are not spiritualizing matter, we are not materializing Spirit: we are living in a spiritual Universe right now.

We are merely experiencing the Universe in which we live. We free ourselves from the thraldom of our own superstition, ignorance, fear, and sense of isolation from the central flame. We call it the Man of the Heart; Jesus called it "the light that lighteth every man's path."† As we go on, let us seek, individually and collectively, more and more to develop a very intimate relationship with the indwelling whatever-you-want-to-call-it. I believe that God is an overdwelling Presence, a universal Presence; but I believe this universal Presence is, within each one

*Perhaps referring to John 1:13.
†Perhaps John 12:35.

of us, the person that we are. I think this is the secret of life: *the overdwelling Presence is the indwelling Person.* Therefore even the Infinite is personal to me in a unique way.

I have a Secret Place, you have a Secret Place, where the Universe presents itself to us fresh and new and lovely, and in transcendent beauty, and in a light so bright that we cannot conceive it—but it is a light different from the light of the sun. "There is in the Universe around us that which responds to us, in the rock and the brook, from the tree and the wind and the wave." Let us identify it. This was the genius of Walt Whitman.

There is that within us which is the eternal Presence as its own Son; it was this with which Meister Eckhart identified himself. There is that within us which is God as His Son and the Son of God as God. It was with this supreme Reality that Jesus identified himself. If it happens to be true—and I believe it is—that there has to be a constant cooperation on our part before this divine consummation can transpire in our individual and collective experience, then it will be our consent through our efforts, through our attention, through our listening—but without sadness and without tears and without weight and without burden. In those transcendent moments everything becomes weightless.

This is real—not a word picture; and so let us get together with the interior Reality of ourselves. Very few people realize it. Religious Science teaches and gives to the world—and it will someday know it—the most transcendent concept of the personalness of God in the life of the individual that has ever been put into print since time began. We do not teach that God is a principle (we teach

that electricity is a principle and that there is a Law of
Mind in action which is another principle): we teach a
transcendent Presence and an immanent Presence and a
very close, warm, colorful relationship not between the
two but the interplay of the One in, around, and upon
Itself. And in those moments of transcendence you will
see everything bathed in Its light. You will hear that
which is behind all music; you will feel that "whatever-
it-may-be"; there is no name for it, but you will feel a
force playing around you on its level and on its plane, as
real as the wind in your face, and you will see all of the
celestial substance. It seems forever to be falling, not *on*
things, but *through everything*—until everything becomes
saturated with it. But you will be more consciously alive
than you ever were before.

Being one who has but heard the slightest echo of this,
caught the slightest gleam of it (Jesus referred to it as the
"pearl of great price"), you will not be satisfied until it
comes more fully orbed. In many experiences I have had,
and know that others may have had, there is nothing
weird, nothing queer. There is nothing peculiar about it.
It is just another extension of what we now are. It takes
in more territory; it encompasses and embodies the center
of your own being. It is another kind of an awareness,
another kind of a get-together-ness.

I think what we have done this week, what we are
doing now, is a prelude to it. I think the time has come
in evolution when many people will step from the pages
of history who will be like the great masters and sages and
saviors. I think we are a product of that evolution which
pushes itself irresistibly forward, urges itself forward, but
never insists. It waits. It has all eternity to wait in.

If we listen, if we stay still long enough, if we accept enough, something will happen to us. That which the good, the great, and the wise proclaimed, and all great religious sytems have been built on, will no longer be heralded by the saviors. *You* will be that savior; *you* will become that Christ; *you* will be that Buddha; *you* will be that Atman. If the theory I have is correct—and I believe it is—each must give his own consent first.

Emerson said, "God will not make Himself manifest through power." I don't think there is any renunciation in it; there is no renunciation in my religion, no denunciation, no lamentation. The whole miserable mess of sin and salvation (two ends of one morbid mistake) will have to be swept from the face of the earth; we will have to get it out of our own consciousness. There is no such thing as the fallen man; there is no such thing as the human apart from the divine. There is no God you and I will ever meet outside that thing, which is in us now, as the immediate Person that we are, the divine Presence we seek to embody. And always, always, there is a voice. It may not be a physical voice—but it comes.

I am the most surprised person among you at what happens in our movement; and I am most delighted. I don't feel I had anything in the world to do with it other than to enjoy and appreciate it, and to companion with you. Let us remember this: the world—our world—has yet to meet the man who has no fear, no morbidity, no denial, no negation in him. Whitman said, "No one has ever worshiped enough; no one has ever adored enough; no one has ever loved enough; no one has ever communed enough." He said that when that divine moment came it "unstopped" him; this thing entered and possessed (but did not obsess) him: he knew of the divinity of all men; he knew that God inhabits everything, flows through everything, and *is* everything.

The message of Jesus is our message to the world. It has never been done before. There is no egotism in it; there is no harshness in it; there is no dogmatism in it: let us keep our movement forever free. We are giving birth to the next great spiritual impulsion of the world—and for the first time in history: free from dogma, fear, superstition, materialism, and all that is built on ignorance and the denial of God. The Universe in which we live is a spiritual system *now*; we are spiritual beings *now*. In such degree as any one of us bears witness in his mind to the "divine fact," the tomb is open and the dead come forth.

This is our mission to the world, this is our message. Never forget it. The world is waiting. Waiting, longing, hoping causes the mind of every living soul to sing the same song. There is something listening to and striving toward that which it knows exists, and it is our office in joy, in peace, in communion, and in the sweetness of friendship to so live, to so love, to so aspire, and to so realize. The transformation takes place *here*. You don't have to wonder if it will take place *out there*; the world will come when enough of us see through the night into that celestial light "that shineth more and more, unto the perfect day."

We are the children of that light. God is real, personal to you and to me, to be communed with. "Speak to Him, then, for he hears./ And spirit with Spirit shall meet./ Closer is He than breathing,/ Nearer than hands and feet." We shall have to speak to Him in each other and embrace Him in each other and love Him in each other—

in the child at play and the baby drinking from the fountain of nature and the young man and the chorus of angels in one grand accord—that the Eternal may itself go forth through us anew into its own creation.

I wouldn't dare to try to tell you how much I think of you, because I am too sentimental. I love you very much and appreciate very much your love. It is the thing to me that is worthwhile.

Now let us turn deep, deep within, to your God and my God—to our Father in our Heaven—that infinite and ineffable Beauty that paints the rose and spreads its glory across the hilltops as the sun rises to bathe the valley in the warmth and color and radiance of a new day; that inhabits the soft twilight shadows in the rose at hues of evening and the song of the lark and the laughter of children and the peace of the night—eternal and forever blessed. We are that which Thou art, and Thou art that which we are.*

Amen.

*See *The Science of Mind* 423:3 for Holmes' use of this expression from the opposite perspective.

CHAPTER 9

Practical Transcendentalism

This talk, given to the Tuesday Invitational group on May 26, 1959, was intended to be the last talk of the year. Ernest was now excited about the imminent completion of Founder's Church. He referred to it as "the symbol of the national movement."

I had mixed emotions as I listened to him. Not too long before this talk he had told his spiritual daughter, Peggy Lee,* in a trip to Palm Springs, that there were only three things he had to do and then he was ready to join his wife, Hazel†:

1. Complete the new church.
2. Dedicate the new organ to Hazel Holmes' memory.
3. Correct the thinking of several people in the Religious Science movement.

He completed the first two of these self-imposed goals. Regrettably, he never got to the third. I have always wondered: if he had, where would Religious Science be in the world of religion today?

---

*The popular singer. She gives a warm account of her relationship with Dr. Holmes and Dr. Bendall in her autobiography, *Miss Peggy Lee.*
†d. 1957.

L AST WEEK, I talked about the general theory back of all of the greatest spiritual perceptions the world has ever had. I had to abbreviate it very much. There was a man here who is a student of philosophy; he is majoring in it to teach it. He asked if you people knew what I was talking about. I said, "Of course. Why else would they be there?" and then he said, "I didn't know there was any group of laymen in the world who could be talked to the way you talked to them." Of course, he would not find them anywhere else except in a university.

Few people know how to think abstractly, and having thought abstractly, they do not know how to apply the abstraction to that which is concrete. Troward said that the broader we generalize, the more completely we can specialize. Emerson said, "The possibility of the elevation of the apex is determined by the base of the structure."

We came to the conclusion that if there is any truth that is known—or if we may accept, with validity, truth that is known—we would have to accept, in philosophy, spiritual things, and, in the general concept of life, that those people who have so accepted are few. In Ouspensky's* *Tertium Organum*, at the end, he tells us that Dr. Bucke, who wrote *Cosmic Consciousness*, said that there was a certain group of spiritual and intellectual elders who appeared throughout the ages, and all of them (from standpoint of number) could be put "in a modern drawing-room."

They have so completely influenced the thought of the world that the highest and best in religion, philosophy,

*P. D. Ouspensky (1878–1947), Russian philosopher and writer on abstract mathematical theory.

and education has come through this group, who appeared over a period of thousands of years. I think that most interesting. Moses would have been one; Lao-tzu would have been another—as would Buddha, Emerson, Kant, Spinoza, and probably Troward. But Bucke was remarking on the fact that a few people had made such a large contribution and exerted so much influence, directly or indirectly, and that the teachings of those few had spread out through larger groups, and so on.

We know that, in the New Thought movement, Emma Curtis Hopkins taught practically all the greatest leaders of the last 50 years. She taught the people who started the Divine Science church and those who started the Unity movement.* Practically all of the leaders of the New Thought movement came under the influence of this one person, and I think that is a very interesting thing. She was an illumined soul, and everything she taught is in the book *High Mysticism*. You have to get used to the language, because her whole theme, discourse, was really: where is your vision set? Jesus asked, "What went ye forth for to see?"

It is an interesting thing that Bucke should say a drawing-room would contain the number of people who have thus influenced the world—not necessarily by a direct teaching, but by teaching people who went out and taught what they taught—and that it is all traceable back to these very few people. Consequently, if we find out

---

*Mrs. Hopkins taught neither the founder of Divine Science—Malinda Elliott Cramer (San Francisco)—nor the co-founders of the affiliated activity in Denver (the Brooks sisters). Dr. Holmes was reliant on the hearsay that has long constituted much of New Thought history.

what these very few people were talking about (which is what we talked about last week—and we do know what they were talking about), then we have the essence of the spiritual wisdom of the world. But we do not necessarily understand the implications of its meaning.

I remember an old man coming up to speak to me after I had talked to Rabbi Trattner's* group one day about the Ark of the Covenant. He asked me where I had gotten the information and things I said, particularly when I told him I was not a Jew. I said, out of many books—because I was interested in that sort of thing. Dr. Trattner said the man was the greatest Jewish scholar on the Pacific Coast. This came into my experience to show that way back there were these great thinkers of the ages who transmitted their thoughts to their people—no matter what denomination you call them (and God doesn't know the difference between any of them).

We will have to go to these original sources to find out what is known to the human mind that translates its experience into transcendent terms—an ever-ascending scope and greater possibility. There would be no group of people on earth who have ever lived, other than these few, as original sources—who Bucke said have influenced the thought of the world more than everything else put together.

Steinmetz† said, before he passed on, that the next hundred years' investigation into what he called psychic (mental and subjective) and spiritual truths would produce more progress in evolution than the last 7000 years

---

*Ernest R. Trattner, rabbi of Westwood Temple, Los Angeles, and friend of Ernest Holmes.
†Charles Steinmetz (1865–1923), American (German-born) electrical engineer.

in human history—and that is quite a statement from a man of his day. He is right, because there is something that opens up; there are certain things that happen in consciousness that you cannot talk to just everybody about. You can talk *at* them, but not *to* them—because there is no communication. You know this is true.

Let's briefly recapitulate what we have talked about, because I would like to speak about its application. Although a transcendent theory is not necessarily the best thing for us, it *is* necessary, in my estimation. I don't believe anyone speaks with authority or with power on any subject unless he knows the subject, and unless there is so much more in the background that he can say, that the people heed what he says and get what he knows by proximity.

Did you read Vincent Sheean's book *Lead Kindly Light*, on the life of Gandhi? He speaks about the thing between Gandhi and the audience, which they called *darshan*, which is a third thing that is established as a result of the contact of the consciousness of the audience and whoever is speaking to them. Unless that happens to some degree —I think it happens in a political talk or any talk that is good—then nothing happens to the audience; but when it happens, something happens to the audience and to the speaker which is transcendent of anything either one of them would independently experience.

It is what people got from Jesus; what one got from Emma Curtis Hopkins. Sometimes I felt it very definitely as a breeze in my face—I am psychic and know the difference between what we call a breeze in a seance and what I am talking about now. This is warm and colorful; it is an entirely different thing. It emanates from a different thing, a different state of mind, of consciousness, and looses a different kind of energy. Nor is all subjective energy necessarily good to experience.

They all have taught the one thing. It doesn't matter whether it is the Jewish Bible, our Bible (of course, the Jewish Bible is our Bible up to the New Testament); they have all taught in one way or another the incarnation—what we call the divine incarnation—except in Christianity they got it all confused and thought it only had to do with Jesus. The divine incarnation didn't have anything more to do with Jesus than the amount of it he permitted to take place consciously—which probably was a great deal of it.

Eckhart said, "God never had but one Son; but," he added, "the Eternal is forever begetting His only-begotten, and He is begetting him in me now." This is heresy, according to some religions. God never had but one Son: if there is only one Father, there can only be one Son; but the Son can appear in many ways. There is only one sonship, generic man, Atman, Buddha, or Christ: "God never had but one Son; but the eternal is forever begetting His only-begotten, and He is begetting him in me now."

This is in line with the teaching of the ages, which we call progressive evolution. "Ever as the spiral grew,/ He left the old house for the new." But a progressive evolution is merely that which mathematically and irresistibly follows what was once a spontaneous involution. You can only get out of the bag what is in it. Nothing will ever evolute that isn't first involuted. But since there is a continual process of involution, there is a corresponding and continual process of evolution.

This is the esoteric meaning of the Tree of Life, which was described as a tree rooted in the ground growing up into the heavens and an inverted tree rooted in Heaven growing down until its branches mingle with the first; and what it meant was this: that as there is something involuted in generic man—man as universal—which *pushes* him up, there is something continually descending into him which *lifts* him up.

I think Lloyd Douglas,* who wrote *White Banners,* must have understood this, because somewhere in it toward the end, the question is asked, "Which is the greater, the push or the pull?" And he said, "They are equal." I think he had to have a pretty good understanding to have said that. In other words, this is Jacob's ladder ascending and descending; there is that always flowing into us which forever tends to flow back into itself. And as Troward said, since you are dealing with an infinite, the point of saturation is never reached.

There are beings beyond us as we are beyond tadpoles. In a progressive evolution, there would have to be. But a progressive evolution is the result of the *conscious* (this is meaning of divine incarnation); it has nothing to do with our theology, the Virgin Birth, the Immaculate Conception—which don't mean anything to anyone who has any sense—and don't worry about it: every conception is immaculate; everything is a virgin birth, whether it is a potato or Topsy.

But there is a truth—an esoteric or hidden truth—back of all these fables and allegories, back of all the teachings and bibles of the world. There is a terrific truth, but it is put in this form to conceal the truth from the average person, thinking that when he was ready, he would get it— which is probably true; but it wouldn't be true in our day

*(1877–1951), American Congregational clergyman and novelist.

145

and age. We seek all the knowledge and wisdom and learning we can get, because we need it so badly.

The whole teaching is that this is known as the descent of the Spirit into matter, and in our theology it would be Lucifer thrown over the embankments of Heaven and landing like a flaming sword on the earth. This is a word picture, telling us that the mundane clod is impregnated with a cosmic spark. That is all it means. There wasn't any devil, or big row, and they didn't throw him overboard—he has no existence, therefore he didn't land anywhere. This is merely a story, like the allegory of Eden. There wasn't any Adam and there wasn't any Eve, but the story depicts a process through which people go in their ignorance, having to learn by experience to return to the state of Eden.

Now, self-conscious individuation no longer is subject to the law of chance and change and the vicissitudes of fortune—like Jesus, who definitely and deliberately said, "I know where I came from; how I got here; why I am here; where I am going; and how to get there. And there isn't anything you have to do about it." He sort of scorned the thought that they could do anything. He said, "You can only do with me what I will." In my estimation, he could have caused his physical body to disappear and they couldn't have found him; and he might have caused theirs to, but he wasn't vicious.

What would happen to any person where the divine spark was completely loosed into action? Would it carry with it not only the Essence and Presence, but the power that is back of everything, and the force that is induced? All words will have some power; some words will have all power, in my estimation. Now, the power is already resident; there would be no creation, because there is only one of whatever there is. It has to include what you and I call Spirit, Soul, Body, Mind, matter—everything. It is not alien to anything: there is no place where God is not; there is no such thing as something which is not already impregnated with the divine Life. This is the meaning of the burning bush. Moses was aware of That in Nature which speaks. This is beyond illusion; you cannot explain it to anyone; because unless they have had it, they don't know what you are talking about. But it is real.

We go back, then, to the divine spark in everything and in everyone; and this spark is God. It is more than a spark, although we call It a spark. Because of the indivisibility of the whole, It is circumferenced nowhere and centered everywhere. It has to be. All of It is present in Its entirety wherever our thought rests. Now, this is a stupendous concept; it is logically and mathematically true, and one of the great teachings of the ages. "I behold in thee the image of him who died on the tree," Lowell said. That is what he found after his search for the Holy Grail.* It is what Jesus understood: "Who hath seen me hath seen the Father. The Father and I are one, yet the Father is greater than I."

It is this divine spark in us, this universal Life in us, this God in us, this Atman—whatever you want to call it. The Truth or Reality automatically had to contain, by the very nature of its being, everything that was going to happen in the processes of evolution to the time when "the divine spark first ignited the mundane clod," from which there evolved that which became man, who finally

*In *The Vision of Sir Launfal.*

stood up and looked about him and said, "I am not my environment." The poetry of each in his own tongue is so beautiful.

This is why Jesus said, "The Father worketh until now, but now I work." What he is trying to explain is what they have all taught: the passage of the divine into whatever you want to call it, containing, as Whitman said, "the seed of perfection at the center of everything" —till what we call the "fall" in Christian theology, which I don't like, because man didn't fall, since there wasn't anywhere for him to fall to, and he won't rise, because there isn't anything for him to rise to. Let's say he fell asleep and will awake—isn't that better? The harshness of the theological connotation of the hellishness that people believe in is too crude for a gentle soul to accept. It has no element of beauty; it has no atmosphere of mysticism. It is cold and brittle and harsh and mean; and don't accept it—because it isn't true.

There is a greaty beauty; and, as Plotinus said, its beauty is terrific. Emerson said, "Ineffable is its beauty," transcendent; but that which was involuted, that which was planted—the seed, the genesis of all creation—had to contain that which pushed, compelled, impelled arbitrarily, automatically, the instrumentality evoluting to the point of its self-conscious life. It had to do it; it couldn't help it, because it is an irresistible force backed up by an immutable will existing in the consciousness of an infinite Something that knows nothing but itself. It cannot be frustrated—God will never have a neurosis; and neither will people when they know God. I think all psychiatrists should be spiritual people. I wouldn't send anyone to a pyschiatrist who was a materialist: he would do them more harm than good. You can only become whole when you get to what is whole. Now, I belive in psychiatry. I believe in anything that works. Anything that will work is good.

But what we are discussing had to contain that which automatically, mechanically, arbitrarily pushed the evolving instrumentality—and that is man—through the period of ignorance, let us say, until there emerged that which now consciously cooperates with the Principle and Presence of its own being. "The Father worketh until now, but now I work." And that is what it means.

Now in all probability, in time (as we measure time—which has no existence other than as the measurement of a sequence of events in a unitary wholeness) when the "face" is turned from the "clod" (the arbitrary and mechanical impulsions of the evolutionary principle, other than those things, we will say, like the automatic stuff in the body that keeps the blood circulating and heart going, and things we don't think about—and if we don't think about them, we are better off), the clod would keep going, but the will and volition and choice and return of affection—let us say, the "communication" —would not be there until the evolving instrumentality became aware of itself. That is why in the East it is called self-realization —the self must raise the self by the self, which is true, and Christian theology says we are saved by grace. They are probably both right. I would put the two together, because grace is the givingness of life, and *that* certainly is given automatically; but we are only saved by using it. The self must raise the self by the self, because the self is God.

Now, if in the background of the cosmic process of involution and evolution there was that which shoved man in his evolution—no one man but all men in all creation—to a point of differentiation of self-perception in a unified field which is equally and evenly distributed everywhere, whose center is everywhere and whose circumference is nowhere, then there is that in us which is still going to further evolution. I mean it is already here. That is why everything is from within, out—that which brought life to the point where man could get up and say, "I am not a dog or a cat; I don't know *what* I am, but I am *something*." And we are still saying that.

That which made us reach that point must have infinite variations and limitless reaches of other points to which it will ultimately bring us. "Eye hath not seen nor ear heard, neither have entered into the heart"—much less the intellect. But there will have to be that within us, right now, already, which is the future evolution of our own soul.

But the next important thing never to forget is that this has all gone through the process of endless eons of time—Emerson said, "So careful of the type it seems, so careless of the single life." It has gone through an endless process of time, because it was subject to the ignorance of time, birth, decay, and death. There is no logic which would lead us to suppose that in a timeless Universe the element of time is anything other than what it took to get where we were going, which we called a place.

What I am trying to say is that from now on—and this is the next great teaching of the ages (what Troward called "entering into the fourth kingdom" or fifth)—future evolution is *conscious cooperation*. If there is already something in us which can turn the water into wine, there is that in us right now which has been awakened in some people like Jesus, Buddha, and others. But it awakened out of *what they were*, not what was in store for them "up there" by a divine providence or a special gift or dispensation. None of these things exist.

God did not pat Mary Baker Eddy on the shoulder. (He did and he didn't.) He is patting *everybody* on the shoulder—but maybe *Mary* listened. He didn't drag Joseph Smith out to look under a rock and dig out something.* (He did and he didn't.) He didn't come to Jesus and say, "You are a nice little Jewish boy and I am going to show you stuff I haven't shown the rest of them—even Isaiah." (He did and he didn't.) He didn't come to Steinmetz and say, "I am going to show you something I didn't show the rest." (But he did.) He didn't tell Einstein, "I am going to tell you things about numbers nobody else ever knew, not even Pythagoras."† But he did tell him—because the Universe is forever imparting itself to its creation; "the Spirit seeketh such"—it can't help it. There is a pressure against everything, whether we call it the libido or divine Urge or Cosmos.

It is the same thing as an irresistible expression of pressure. But since we have come to a point of self-determination, the pressure is an *impulsion*. There is always a witness; there is always something saying, "There is more; behold!" There is always something saying, "You can, I can, we can"—always. There is always the thing in us that is transcendent and triumphant. "My head, though bloodied, is unbowed." There is always that which is prophetic of the future—prophetic physically, psychically, and spiritually—always. It is always there.

Therefore it is written in the Book of Life in our own

---

*(1805–1844), founder of the Mormon church, who claimed to have excavated a book (*The Book of Mormon*) written on golden plates.
†(ca.580–ca.500 B.C.), Greek philosopher and mathematician.

soul what we are going to be*; and since we know this, our evolution by conscious cooperation should be much more rapid. In a timeless Universe there is no reason, theoretically, why you and I should not know now; but something in us *does* know what is going to happen to us a million years from now. I don't know whether it is valuable to know; I am not anxious even to try to find out. But the theory of the thing is correct, like a mathematic progression; but we would arrive at it and not understand its meaning.

It would be perfectly normal for a person to understand how to dematerialize his body and appear in New York and materialize it; it wouldn't be strange; it isn't crazy or silly; it has been done in our generation, regardless whether anybody did it exactly that way. I have had experiences where things passed through a wall. I don't know *how* they got through—*but it happened*; and nothing happens outside the realm of law and order. Our reaction to it may be that it is crazy, but that isn't so: it has to do with something in ourself that is there, but we don't understand it; we don't realize it.

There is no reason why we shouldn't take part in our conscious evolution. This is the practical application of the wisdom of the ages, which the ages did not realize until the present age—the last 100 years.† Something new then happened, not *to* the process of evolution—nothing can ever happen *to* it—but *in* the process of evolution which loosed a different kind of cosmic power. It had to happen some time. It happens to have happened in the

---

*Perhaps a reference to 1 John 3:2.
†Beginning with the full maturity and closing years of P. P. Quimby.

last 125 years,* and as a result of it, we have all these metaphysical movements—and they are still very much disturbed for fear one is stealing from the other, etc. What a lack of grandeur of concept!

Someone called me and wanted to quote something I had said, and I said, "All right"; and they said they would give me credit—and then I said, "No, don't quote it: if it is true, it doesn't belong to me; and if it isn't, you shouldn't be repeating it." How can truth belong to anyone? Who owns beauty? It just can't be done; and it is only the one who gives all that gets all.

Now, the practical application of the cosmic reality is something new in the world. Remember this. It is something in our psychology. People like David Seabury know about it, and I have met a number† who do; but psychology as such knows nothing about it and doesn't believe in it. It is something that even medicine—which I think is much nearer to divine Reality than theology—does not. And I am a great admirer of medicine, because what can be better than something that relieves people from suffering? Anyone in our field who criticizes it is silly.

Every truth belongs to *all* truth. It is something only the idealistic philosophers, and only the top grade of them, can understand. They *will* understand it if they ever understand the philosophic and spiritual implications of Einstein's theory that energy and mass are the same thing. Our whole theory is based on the assumption that we are living in a spiritual Universe right now, governed by laws of intelligence. Intelligence, moving, acts as law. The

*Beginning ca. 1838 with Quimby's serious investigation of the phenomena of mesmerism.
†I.e. of psychologists.

153

Universe contains not only a will, but a force, an energy, an action. It is its nature to continuously express itself in form. There is no barrier. There is nothing but it. God is everything.

Our whole practice rests on the theory that mind and matter are equal, identical, and interchangeable, just like Einstein's concept that energy and mass are equal, identical, and interchangeable—because a thought or a mental or spiritual treatment could not reach that which is alien to its own field, could it? It could only reach that which is like itself. This is why Quimby said, "Mind is matter in solution, matter is mind in form" and that there is a superior wisdom, of which these two are as the matter of Spirit, and that use of this is the Science of Christ. It is true, and this is where we get that expression.

Therefore our whole theory is based on the assumption that everything is a mental formation in the Universe— the planets, everything. We don't deny their reality. We don't say people don't have the mumps and measles; but *what are they*? We don't say it isn't good to do anything that will relieve them; but we say we have a specialized field. Yet we are interested in all the fields. We believe in them and in anything that works. Certainly there should be no derision—nothing that even contains the slightest degree of condemnation of something we know nothing about. Modern medicine is a great thing, as are modern surgery and psychiatry. We admire them and admit it, if we have to. We do not hesitate to use them. They are all right; nothing wrong with them. But we have the equal privilege, prerogative, opportunity—and, I think, *necessity* for our own evolution—to recognize that there is something else.

The Universe is not limited to what we call matter or physical form, or to the mind that molds it. There is something in us that can think differently. It certainly is not limited to what it has done or to what it seemed or appeared to have been. And who shall set any limit to the transcendency or to the possibility, mathematically and logically, of that greater Thing? And who shall say to you or to me, "You couldn't do it"? No one. This is where we do not desert our tolerance. We should not entertain the intolerance of that which denies our prerogative—because we are lost if we do.

We are working in a transcendent field. We are working in the field of That which makes things out of Itself by Itself becoming what It makes by a process instinctive and inherent in the constitution and nature of Its own being. It doesn't borrow from anywhere. A spontaneous proclamation of Itself into form, an eternal creativity, implies the necessity of an eternal creation.

All creation is the logical and inevitable necessity of a creator. You will find that in the statement of convictions I wrote one time. It is self-evident, and the great minds of all the ages have known it. It has to be that way.

Now, we must not deny ourselves the privilege of working in a transcendent field, to which the visible is subject by the law of that transcendency. There wouldn't be any question in it whether it would be or not. We wouldn't argue with any given fact—as though it had the right to argue back and tell us whether it "would" or "wouldn't." It has nothing to say about it; it exists by proxy; it exists as a shadow of substance. In and of itself it is neither person, place, nor thing; neither law, cause, nor effect.

Plotinus spoke this of all nature. He said, "Nature is the great no thing, but it isn't nothing; it is less than something and more than nothing. Its business is to receive the form of the contemplation of the thought of the Spirit." If you could talk to the First Cause and say, "How do you create?" it would say, "I create by self-contemplation, and as I think or know or meditate, I let fall the forms of my thought into this whatever-they-call-it."

Lao-tzu said, "All things are possible to him who can perfectly practice inaction." But he is talking about an action whose intensity is infinite compared to our highest concept of movement. He is talking about the inaction in which all action takes place—"Be still, and know that I am God"; "Look unto me, and be ye saved, all the ends of the earth"; "I will look up unto the hills from whence cometh my help."

So we seek the direct, personal, and collective application of a universal Principle backed by a universal Presence. The Principle is a universal power whose nature it is forever to take form and forever to dissolve the form it has taken. Nothing is permanent. If it were, everyone would get caught in a trap, and evolution would cease then and there.

Someone said to me the other day, "Probably when you were a boy things were more stable and didn't change so much." And I said, "Yes, but never forget: you haven't an atom in your body you had a year ago." Everything out here is like a river flowing; you can't jump in the same river twice. You can never return to the same point in mind where you were. There is no such person as in the photograph that was taken ten years ago. It's a picture in loving memory, but there isn't such a person.

If you go back to the old swimming hole where you swam as a kid, you'll find nothing is the same but the hole; what you swam in rushed on long ago to meet the undifferentiated sea or ocean of its own being, to be caught up again and be precipitated in another hole. There is no permanency but change, and if there were, we would all be caught in the traps of the inexorable and the immutable. So we don't need to be afraid of change. It is just a question of the direction in which the change is taking us: to a greater liberation or toward a bondage (which will only be temporary).

There is no such thing as good and evil in the Universe, no such thing as right and wrong, no such thing as God and man, no such thing as a manifest Universe separate from what manifests it—the manifestation is the Manifester in the manifestation. It is not strange to me that Moses talked to a burning bush. Everything has a soul and responds. You can talk to a plant and have it spring into newness.

You and I are practicing in a transcendent field. We understand it. We are not going to argue with anyone who knows nothing about it, as to whether or not it is true. Who cares what anyone thinks about what I believe? I used to have a motto which said, "The great are great to us only because we are on our knees. Let us arise." You are the only great person you will ever meet; you are the only soul you will ever know; within you is the only God you will ever contact. Out of this thing which the Universe has seen fit to manifest because of Its own nature, with which you and I have nothing to do, comes the future of your evolution—and from nowhere else.

So now let us know, as we break for the summer in joy and gladness, grateful for the privilege of this communion of spirit, soul, and mind, this closeness of even that which is physical: there shall be warmth and color that emanate and embrace us all on all the planes of existence. They are all real, good, and wonderful; they all belong or they wouldn't be here; we *do* belong to the Universe. And as we give back to That which has endowed us with it, It shall again give back on the same circuit that which will still further accentuate the essence of our own being, until finally, looking up, we see God only.

So it is.

CHAPTER 10

The Soul of Ernest Holmes

Dr. Holmes loved poetry of all kinds. He avidly read it and quoted it in his talks. He recited it to us in the intimacy of his own home. When he and his brother Dr. Fenwicke Holmes got together, at the urging of Fenwicke, to write *The Voice Celestial*, he was overjoyed. However, Fenwicke was in San Francisco and Ernest in Los Angeles. Ernest would send his contribution to Fenwicke, and much of Ernest's simple sensibility would be lost in the process.

Ernest had an idea and wrote something that he retained for Fenwicke's next visit to see if it could be included in the book. He read it to the Tuesday Invitational meeting of February 4, 1959, when he talked about basic prayer work.* Fenwicke didn't want it, and not too many of the Tuesday group responded enthusiastically, so he gave the original copy to me, saying, "You like it, and I like it, so you can have it."

It is fitting that this first volume of *The Holmes Papers*, reflecting the philosophy of Ernest Holmes, include this, which he called "A Fable."

---

*See "Basic Treatment Work," in *The Anatomy of Healing Prayer*, vol. 2 of *The Holmes Papers*, pp. 173–183.

A FABLE

Time stretched in the arms of Eternity and yawned—longing for liberation from its bondage—it was tired of doing nothing.

Eternity embraced both Time and the Timeless—holding them fondly to itself lest it be without offspring;

But all three of them—Time, Eternity and the Timeless—were weary with the monotony of inaction;

And so they held a conference to see if they might not find some way to come to a solution of their desires.

Not knowing just how to proceed, since they had but little mind of their own, they decided to consult the Old Man of the Mountains—the Self-Existent One—who possessed the Apple of Wisdom.

So they journeyed into the Mountains where the Old Man lived and laid their problem before him.

The Old Man received them graciously and promised them to do whatever was in his power to help; together they held long conferences, but it was difficult for them to come to any conclusion.

Eternity was not particularly concerned, having been around for a long while, and being used to his own company and not lonesome—except for those periods when he wondered if he were not dreaming the eons away;

But Time and the Timeless were most impatient indeed— they just couldn't wait; for, you see, neither of them were beings in themselves; they both lived by a sort of reflected glory from Eternity—while Eternity depended on the Old Man of the Mountains for its life.

Now of course this was why they were having a conference.

The Old Man looked across space and down on Chaos and Old Night and said: My beloved children, I just want to make you happy; I can understand you do not wish to be waiting around for countless ages with nothing to do, so I have decided to grant you some powers which until now you have not enjoyed.

But first I must move upon the Face of the Deep and disturb Chaos and Old Night. Heaven knows they have been asleep long enough—I had almost forgotten them—they really are a strange pair, sort of lawless at that—almost, but not quite, beings—*things* they are, with no minds of their own. I suppose I will have to breathe some kind of law into them so when they get stirred up they will not destroy themselves; but I will put some kind of order in them so they can be playthings for Eternity; then he will not be bothering me with his ideas about creating things—he just can't seem to sit still and enjoy himself.

To which the Timeless answered by saying he felt almost as Eternity did; he couldn't see any sense at all in waiting and waiting and waiting and having nothing to do.

To which little Time peeped up with a very small voice indeed, saying he too had waited for something to happen—he almost wished he had a mind of his own and was not compelled to live on the Timeless.

The Timeless responded by saying that in many ways he was in a worse condition than Time, because he was so much bigger and more important—which of course he would have to be since he furnished the background for Time to play in—and Eternity, who felt himself to be the Father of both Time and the Timeless, said he would go along with the idea.

So it was agreed between Time and the Timeless that they would work together—Time as the child of the Timeless—and Time was given power to be unhindered, almost but not quite, because the Timeless never would wish to be in the position of being bound by Time, who was prone to get into all sorts of trouble and might get caught up in what he was doing, and then nothing but confusion would follow—which it almost did, but not quite.

And it was agreed that the Timeless would cooperate with Eternity, because all three of them—Time, Eternity and the Timeless—were one family, really, and would have to work together.

So Eternity agreed to free the Timeless from its bondage, and the Timeless agreed to free Time so it might act somewhat on its own.

Now all these discussions took place in the Mountains where the Old Man lived who possessed the Apple of Wisdom.

The Old Man said he was quite happy where he was and never did wish to limit himself to anything in particular; but he did agree that he would find a lot of pleasure in watching the actions of Eternity, Time and the Timeless.

But he cautioned Eternity and its offspring, Time and the Timeless, telling them they must never do anything that would destroy his peace, because the Old Man didn't wish to be bothered.

Eternity agreed to keep faith with the Old Man: he merely wanted to partake of his wisdom; he didn't expect to act entirely on his own.

The Old Man agreed to give Eternity as much freedom as was necessary for it to set Time in motion, and Eternity agreed to pass on some of the power the Old Man bestowed on him to the Timeless, that it might activate Time.

Time, Eternity and the Timeless were very impatient to get started—but the Old Man motioned them to wait while he meditated—and the Old Man sat in thoughtful silence for a long time, once in a while eating from the Apple of Wisdom, which was never consumed, and in his meditations every once in a while he would smile and nod to himself, as though he were very satisfied with what was taking place in his mind—and finally he said: My children, I have an idea to put before you:

Let us create Beings and a place where they can function and live in happiness and freedom, but bound to us with enduring ties that can never be loosed.

Time, Eternity and the Timeless laughed with delight and danced around the Old Man, clapping their hands with joy.

Eternity said: I will gladly give birth to such Beings for you and will guard them very carefully, holding them always in my embrace, just as I have Time and the Timeless—and bowing before the Old Man, he thanked him for his wisdom.

But the Timeless was not quite so certain, while Time was really quite impatient with the whole affair, which he always had been from the beginning.

But after much discussion, they decided to try the experiment and see what would happen. But just how to begin, Eternity, Time and the Timeless did not quite know—which they couldn't, because they themselves were always subject to the will of the Old Man.

And again the Old Man ate from the Apple of Wisdom, which never diminished, and after a long while he unfolded a plan to them which he thought would work.

The Old Man said: In creating such Beings as these I have in mind, it will be necessary for me to impart some of my own life to them—which was reasonable enough, since the Old Man didn't have anything to make them out of but himself.

And so he explained to Eternity, Time and the Timeless that these Beings he was about to create would have to be a little different from them, since they had no real life of their own, and no mind with which to create ideas, and no power except it were borrowed from him—for after all, they were but reactions of the Old Man's thoughts and ideas, enjoying freedom only in certain limits.

But the Beings the Old Man was about to create—he explained to them—would have within themselves certain qualities which the Old Man possessed. But he would hide these qualities so deep in their beings that they would at first be quite unconscious of them, for they had a long journey ahead of them before they could ever return to the Old Man and consciously cooperate with him.

Now here was something indeed difficult—or it would be difficult for finite Beings—but the Old Man, eating again from the Apple of Wisdom which never seemed to be consumed, continued his meditations and finally said: Lest the Beings I am about to create would immaturely try to act on their own, I must create some kind of a cloud between them and myself so they will not be able to see me exactly as I am, because I am going to endow them with my own being—they will always have a curiosity and an urge to return again to me, because they can never really be whole until they do this—but should they seize the power I am going to endow them with before they know how to use it, they might fall into all kinds of confusion—which they certainly did.

So the Old Man reaffirmed that while he was going to impart his own nature to these Beings he was about to create, he would sort of let them alone to discover themselves and gradually to come under the Eternal Laws of his being—but the time of this would not be known to them—but of course the Old Man knew, since he knew everything, because he possessed the Apple of Wisdom.

He said he would move upon Chaos and Old Night and breathe some kind of law into them which would reflect back to the Beings he was about to create the images of their own thinking, like a mirror; and since their own thinking would be pretty chaotic to start with—and for a long time to come—they would look at these images—which were really reflections of their own minds—and mistake them for realities. But always there would be thoughts and ideas of the Old Man moving down through the cloud he would create to almost separate himself from these beings —but not quite; there would always be thoughts and ideas of the Old Man showing something through the cloud; and because he was endowing these Beings with certain qualities of his own nature, they would always be looking up as though they expected to discover something that would make them more complete and happy.

And so, you see, above these Beings would be the cloud through which the thoughts of the Old Man would be reflected down toward them, and they would feel these thoughts and ideas—because they were also within them; and because the Old Man would put some of his being into them, they too would have a certain kind of creativity which would reflect itself on the lower side of the cloud and all around them —because all the earth then would act like a mirror.

Then the Old Man explained to Eternity, Time and the Timeless that there might be quite a period of confusion down there, but it was the only way he knew to create beings that finally could act on their own but still in cooperation with him.

And the long time of their confusion would be called the Period of Ignorance—and gradually as the confusion cleared away and they looked up through the cloud that almost but not quite separated the Old Man from them, they would become more and more like him, and this process of becoming more like him would be called their Enlightenment; and finally as this Enlightenment grew, the cloud would disappear entirely and they would no longer reflect confusion into the great mirror of life, and the mirror would reflect to them only the nature of the Old Man's Being.

The Old Man explained to Time, Eternity and the Timeless that in creating this cloud of unknowing and the
mirror of false appearing* he was creating a medium
which in a sense would bind the Beings he was creating for a period of time, because they would be looking mostly at their own creations and mistaking them
for realities, in that way becoming subject to them.

This would be part of the illusion through which they
would pass in the Period of Ignorance.

And the Old Man said he would breathe on Chaos and
Old Night and endow them with certain qualities
that Time, Eternity and the Timeless did not and
never could possess because they had no initiative of
their own.

So the Old Man breathed two principles into Chaos and
Old Night and endowed them with a certain amount
of creativity: one of the principles would be reflected
back to them, and in their experiences and conditions
that would be like their own thoughts and ideas—
and for a long while they might suffer some results
of their own ignorance because of this; and the time
of this period would be known as "evolution," or
unfoldment of the life he was going to breathe into
them—from complete ignorance, as far as the Beings
were concerned, to gradually awakening to a realization of their own natures.

In other words, the Old Man said: The speck of my own
life with which I am going to endow these Beings will

*See, for example, Metaphysical Chart No. VI in *The Science of
Mind*, p. 574.

lie dormant, but it will always be stirring and stirring and causing these Beings gradually to awaken to a realization of who and what they are.

And during this period the two principles which he breathed into Chaos and Old Night would be reacting to them in accordance with their own thoughts, and these Beings unwittingly, in complete ignorance of their own natures, would be reflecting into this mirror that surrounds them the thoughts and imaginations which some time would prove to be their own undoing—but only for a brief period of time.

And there would come up among them those who, because of a more penetrating gaze, had looked through the cloud and mist and, receiving more intelligence, would look again into the mirror that is around them and become conscious that it was a mirror only, and it would be called a Mirror of the Mind, and the forms it created would be called the Mirror of Matter*—but neither one would be real in itself.

But these Beings would be subject to their own creations until their time of emancipation—and the Old Man explained, because he possessed the Apple of Wisdom and knew all things, that during this period, not because of the spark he was going to breathe into these Beings, which would cause them almost to look up, but because of the inertia of the images around them in the Mirror of Mind and Nature, considerable confusion would follow.

*These terms are discussed in *The Science of Mind*, p. 612.

For the spark with which the Old Man would endow them would always be groping its way through the cloud, and its very Presence would endow these Beings with hope and faith and an inward assurance that they would never become extinct. But because of the confusion around them, they would always be trying to reconcile that which they inwardly felt to what they were experiencing, as a result of the action and reactions in the mirror.

And he said all sorts of different beliefs would arrive among these Beings and distribute their arguments as they tried to adjust themselves to an inward seeming that knew but little about these outward things which would appear to contradict these inward feelings. And these Beings, following an inward knowing with which he was going to endow them, would, without knowing why they did it, announce there was some power that could make them whole. But everywhere they looked, it would seem as though what they said would contradict this. And only those who continuously looked upward through the cloud would really see things as they were, while the rest would be looking at them as they appeared to be.

And great systems of belief would arise, and much discussion and argument and dispute would follow, and these Beings would feel themselves alone and isolated but always speak of the knowledge to be theirs; and as it grew in brilliance and they reached up through the clouds that seemed to obscure their confusion and difficulties, these things would gradually disappear, and with them their fears, uncertainties and doubts.

The Old Man explained that because the life with which he would endow these Beings would have to be some part of himself, they would be eternal, and something in them would always know this.

But here too great arguments would arise: the Beings' confusion would create all kinds of strange beliefs about their destiny, and many of them would be very weird indeed; but this ignorance too would clear away.

The Old Man explained to Time, Eternity and the Timeless that this whole action would take place within them, and that since Eternity was forever, and never could be exhausted or its energies used up, it would not be disturbed very much by the process; and since the Timeless, which itself lived on Eternity, was by Eternity furnished a background for Time, it too would not be greatly disturbed. But little Time would fall into a lot of confusion, because the Beings he was going to create would often mistake Time for Eternity and the Timeless and, being caught in Time, would be bound to its limitations, but only for a period.

And he explained to Time this was why he had told them in the beginning that Time must never really be caught nor the Timeless confined, else Eternity would be bound. He said, You see, Time and the Timeless will be the action and reaction in Eternity; and Eternity itself is merely a reaction to the mind of Beings.

Having carefully explained all these things to Eternity, Time and the Timeless, the Old Man said: Now, my children, it is time for you to return to your homes. But remember this: I have breathed law and order into Chaos and Old Night, and you will never be permitted to do anything that can violate my Beings.

But Eternity was permitted to play with the Timeless, and the Timeless was permitted to play with Time; but none of them would ever be permitted to get caught even in their own actions.

So Time, Eternity and the Timeless, having thanked the Old Man for his generosity, hand in hand left the mountain and journeyed back again, happy with themselves and content with the power the Old Man had bestowed upon them. And having reached the Valley where they lived, and being fatigued because of their long journey, they all felt the need of resting for a while; and so all three of them fell asleep, not quite realizing what the Old Man had done to them.

And sleeping, they dreamed. Time dreamed it was Lord of all creation; the Timeless that it was Lord over all; and Eternity that it was the Father of all. The dream was pleasant enough; but like all dreams, it must come to an end, to be followed by an awakening.

And the waking from this dream is the story of man's evolution.